Dolly's

DESSERTS

There's Always Room for Dessert

CHARLIE SMARK & JANINE DAVIES

Contents

Recipe List

FEELING FRUITY

CHOCOHOLIC

THROWBACKS

BASIC BISCUITS

ICE CREAM

PAMPERED PUPS

FILLINGS AND SPREADS

Welcome!

Hello, everyone, and welcome to the very first Dolly's Desserts cookbook!

We are so excited for you to make some of our store's most popular recipes at home! Whether you're a baking expert or a total beginner, there is something in here for everyone. We've created these recipes to give you a behind-the-scenes look into our world and to help you have some fun with baking! You'll find all your favourite flavours and chocolate bars inside, and our recipes are super easy to adapt, so you can swap and change things out to suit you. This is something we do in store all the time!

Dolly's is a family business, and family is what we are all about. Our book has recipes for everyone - even the dog!

We'd like to thank all our amazing followers! You've seen our company grow over the years and this book wouldn't have been possible without your support!

Enjoy!

UTELLA
ISCOFF
CARAMEL
PEANUT BUTTER
KINDER BUENO

SHAKES

OOKIE DOUGH
HOC BROWNIE
RY CHEESECAKE

Our Story

2016 – THE IDEA

It all began when we embarked on a family holiday to Thailand and saw Thai ice cream rolls. We fell in love with the concept and realised that there wasn't anything like it available in the UK! My mum was dissatisfied with her job at the time, and I had no idea what I wanted to do after college, so we made the decision to venture into business together as a mother-daughter team. Being very naive, we ordered an ice cream pan machine from China and dedicated countless hours to mastering the art of creating ice cream rolls (which was a lot more difficult than we imagined). After persistent efforts, we succeeded in perfecting our recipe, and Ice Queenz was born!

2017 – ON THE ROAD!

During the summer of 2017, we took our ice cream rolls on tour! We visited different food festivals and brought Ice Queenz to customers all across the UK, including our hometown of Barnsley. My mum and dad have worked in Barnsley market all my life, so it just seemed like the perfect place to begin. As the summer drew to a close, we reflected on our success and realised it was time to seek out a more permanent home for Ice Queenz.

2017 – ICE QUEENZ

After discovering the perfect location, we proudly launched our Ice Queenz shop in Barnsley. As the business grew, so did our menu (let's be honest, there was no chance we were just going to sell ice cream in the cold Barnsley winters!). We decided to include other desserts like waffles, crepes and cookie dough, along with coffees and milkshakes.

However, as time went on, we realised that ice cream rolls weren't quite the right fit for us. Truthfully, they were so time-consuming, and we started to feel like we'd outgrown the brand. We wanted to move the business towards a new direction, so we went on a course to master the art of making gelato and fell in love with it! With this newfound passion, we made the decision to transition from ice cream rolls to gelato (and it's the best decision we have ever made!).

2019 – DOLLY'S DESSERTS

Since the Ice Queenz brand was so deeply rooted in the world of ice cream rolls, we decided to rebrand when we made the switch to gelato. Named after our beloved pet cockapoo, Dolly, Mum and I decided to rebrand as Dolly's Desserts.

Our timing couldn't have been better as the construction of Market Kitchen in Barnsley town centre commenced in 2019. Seizing the opportunity, we opened the first Dolly's Desserts location, and this spot remains open today! We closed our Ice Queenz location and opened a kiosk-style location in the Market Kitchen, alongside other independents serving up food from all over the world.

This was where our passion for baking was sparked. We used to buy things in, but we were never 100% happy with the outcome. The decision was made to start baking in our kitchen at home (which felt like the ice cream rolls all over again), and my mum worked tirelessly to tweak our signature brownie recipe until it was perfect. These became a huge hit with our customers, and we started to sell out every week!

Dolly's
DESSERTS

Dolly's

there's always room for
DESSERT

Dolly's
DESSERTS
OPEN

Dolly's
DESSERTS

Dolly's

2020 - CLOSED DOORS

As the Market Kitchen started to get really busy, Dolly's Desserts was growing in popularity in Barnsley. However, when lockdown hit, our operations were brought to an abrupt halt, forcing Dolly's to close its doors indefinitely. Like many small businesses, there was uncertainty over what the future would hold for us as a business.

2021 - ONLINE GROWTH

Amidst the challenges, we decided to pour our time into a brand-new platform: TikTok. Despite the app being in its early stages, we dove into the world of short videos and quickly developed a passion for it. When restrictions eased and businesses could offer takeaway services, this brought a renewed love for TikTok as we could share behind-the-scenes glimpses of our desserts and the inner workings of the business.

The response was amazing – Dolly's TikTok account rapidly gained traction, surpassing over a MILLION followers in no time. People from all corners of the UK started to flock to our store to try our irresistible treats for themselves. As our social media presence continued to grow and the shop became increasingly busy, we wondered how Dolly's could reach even more customers. More and more people were making the journey to Barnsley, always making sure to take away our bakes to share with their loved ones, but we began to wonder about the ones who couldn't make the trip. That's when we decided to launch our online store, and work started on creating products which we could send through the post. Our cookie dough kits were our first product, and they became instant hit!

2022 - EXPANSION

Just when we thought it couldn't get any busier, even more people came to visit Dolly's, leaving queues snaking around the market. Meanwhile, we were still making all the bakes for the shop in our home kitchen. With timing once again on our side, and Barnsley's brand-new Glass Works refurbishment taking place, it became evident that the natural next step would be to open our very own store! From here on, we gave our undivided attention to creating the ultimate Dolly's experience in our sit-down store. We poured our hearts into the shop and built it from the ground up, with every detail being meticulously planned to provide a complete luxury experience. Eventually, in December 2022, just a week before Christmas, we proudly opened the doors, and our vision for Dolly's was brought to life!

2023- DOLLY'S AT HOME

Due to Dolly's large following on TikTok, venturing onto a brand-new shopping platform, TikTok Shop, was a no-brainer. While thinking of new products, we had a brainwave and thought of bottling up our signature sauces, allowing people to elevate any dessert with that special Dolly's touch! The response was overwhelming. Following a hectic Black Friday and Christmas season, thousands of our products were sent from our little shop in Barnsley all across the UK. As 2023 drew to a close, we were astounded by the vast number of people the brand had touched.

2024 - MAKING PLANS

The new year brought new opportunities for our brand, and we began the year with a visit to Italy to learn new skills. With these skills in place, we started making gelato cakes to order, and we continue to experiment, even making a 20-layer gelato cake to sell by the slice! As we've settled into our newest store, we've had some exciting collaborations with brands such as Tango, Nutella, Now TV, Chlomana, and then came the offer to write our very first book... We can't wait to see what the rest of 2024 holds!

If someone told us a year ago that we would have an actual cookbook, we never would've believed them. But here we are with our own cookbook full of sweet treats for everyone to enjoy!

It has been so fun to create all these easy, amazing recipes and to share some of our shop favourites from over the years. We've had a little help from our amazing team members, so we'd like to give a special thanks to Anika, Hattie, Georga, Liv and Tilly for their fantastic recipes and hard work, day in, day out.

If you're reading this, then you've bought our book, so thank you so much! We never thought this would be possible, and your support has helped to make our dreams a reality. Our biggest thanks goes to our dedicated followers – whether you joined us right at the beginning of our journey or only recently, this book wouldn't have been possible without each and every one of you. We are forever grateful for your continued support and for everyone that has watched our journey up until now. We can't wait to see what the future holds!

there's always room for
DESSERT
Dolly's

there's always room for
DESSERT

there's always room for
DESSERT
Dolly's

there's always room for
DESSERT
Dolly's

there's always room for
DESSERT
Dolly's

there's always room
DESSERT
Dolly's

there's always room for
DESSERT
Dolly's

Feeling Fruity

Bursting with colour and vibrant flavours, this chapter features some of our fruity favourites, including our signature pancakes, lazy day brunches, and unique gift ideas like our Luxury Dipped Strawberries. Why not try our Strawberry Shortcake Freakshake to pull out all the stops and impress your friends!

Blueberry & Banana Pancakes

A hearty breakfast for those lazy Sunday mornings. This recipe is so simple to make and a real treat for everyone! We love a blueberry pancake anyway but adding the banana... game changer.

PREP TIME: 5 MINUTES | COOKING TIME: 10 MINUTES | SERVES 4

Ingredients

350g plain flour

2 tsp baking powder

50g granulated sugar

1 tsp salt

350ml milk

2 eggs

75g butter, melted

1 tsp vanilla extract

100g blueberries

2 ripe bananas, cut in slices diagonally

Maple syrup, to serve

Greek yoghurt, to serve

Method

1. Add the flour, baking powder, sugar, salt, and milk to a bowl and whisk.

2. Once fully combined and there are no lumps, add the eggs, melted butter and vanilla. Whisk until it forms a thick, smooth batter.

3. Heat a large pan on a medium heat and add a little butter to stop the pancakes from sticking. Spoon the batter into the pan to make small 3-inch pancakes. (Depending on the size of your pan, you might have to do this a few times until you have used all the batter.)

4. Carefully place the blueberries and banana slices on top of each of the pancakes, then top with a little more batter.

5. When bubbles start to form on top of the pancakes, they are ready to flip. Cook until the pancakes are golden-brown in colour. Repeat with the remaining batter.

6. Place on a plate, drizzle with maple syrup, add a large spoon of greek yoghurt, and enjoy!

Tip: The blueberries in this recipe can be switched out for raspberries!

Cherry Bakewell Blondies

This is one of the prettiest bakes we make - it really does look impressive. We always get requests for them as they are in our postal mystery boxes, and I can see why. They taste as good as they look!

PREP TIME: 10 MINUTES | COOKING TIME: 30 MINUTES | MAKES 9

Ingredients

190g salted butter, melted

125g caster sugar

200g light soft brown sugar

3 eggs

1 tsp almond essence

330g plain flour

200g white chocolate chips

6 cherry bakewell tarts (homemade or shop-bought)

170g glacé cherries

75g flaked almonds

Method

1. Preheat the oven to 180ºc and line a 20x20cm baking tin.

2. In a bowl, mix the melted butter, caster sugar and light soft brown sugar together.

3. Crack in the eggs, add the almond essence, and mix again.

4. Sift in the flour and fold until combined.

5. Melt the white chocolate chips in the microwave and fold them into the mixture.

6. Add half the blondie batter into the baking tray and smooth it out to the edges to create an even layer.

7. Break up the cherry bakewell tarts using your hands and evenly scatter the pieces over the batter. Add half the glacé cherries, scattered over the top, then top with the remaining blondie batter and spread it out to the edges again.

8. Finish with the remaining cherries and flaked almonds, then bake for 25 to 30 minutes until golden brown.

Raspberry & White Chocolate Crepes

One word: wow. These raspberry and white chocolate crepes are the perfect combination of fruity and sweet, with a little touch of tart. Amazing when served as a dessert or a lazy morning brunch.

PREP TIME: 10 MINUTES | COOKING TIME: 20 MINUTES | MAKES 6

Ingredients

FOR THE RASPBERRY COMPOTE

300g fresh raspberries

4 tbsp icing sugar, plus extra to serve

3 tbsp lemon juice

FOR THE CREPES

125g plain flour

Pinch of salt

250ml milk

1 large egg

TO SERVE

Dolly's Luxury White Chocolate Dessert Sauce

Whipped cream (optional)

Method

1. To make the raspberry compote, add the raspberries, icing sugar and lemon juice to a saucepan on a medium heat. Stir for a few minutes until the raspberries break down and the sugar dissolves.

2. Allow to simmer for 10 minutes, stirring every few minutes so it doesn't stick.

3. Once the compote thickens, place it in a small pot and set aside to cool.

4. To make the crepes, whisk the flour, salt and milk together in a bowl.

5. Add the egg and whisk again until fully combined (making sure there are no lumps!).

6. Put a medium-sized non-stick frying pan on a medium heat and add a little bit of butter (honestly, you don't need a lot as you don't want the crepes to be greasy!).

7. Pour a bit of the batter into the pan and swirl it around until the bottom of the pan is coated in the batter. You want a nice, thin crepe.

8. Cook for a minute, then flip! (You can flip it like it's pancake day if you want, but if you wanna play it safe, just use a rubber spatula to flip it.)

9. Once you have a nice colour on your crepe, pop it on a plate and set it aside. Repeat the process with the rest of the batter to make about six large crepes.

10. Serve each crepe with a dollop of raspberry compote, a drizzle of Dolly's White Chocolate Sauce, some whipped cream, and a dust of icing sugar too if you're feeling fancy!

Tip: If you have no Dolly's sauce, any shop-bought melted white chocolate works well, too.

Raspberry Cheesecake Milkshake

Found in the "Dolly's Shakes" section of our in-store menu, this is a firm favourite amongst our customers and is not your typical milkshake. This is a combination of tangy raspberry, homemade ice cream, and buttery biscuit, all wrapped up in one indulgent drink.

PREP TIME: 5 MINUTES | SERVES 2

Ingredients

140ml whole milk

350g vanilla ice cream (shop-bought or homemade, see page 176)

170g cream cheese

2 digestive biscuits, plus one extra to crumble for decoration

230g frozen raspberries

Whipped cream, to serve

Fresh or freeze-dried raspberries (optional)

Method

1. Add the milk, ice cream, cream cheese, 2 digestives and the frozen raspberries to an electric blender and blend until smooth.

2. Divide between 2 glasses then top with whipped cream and the third biscuit, crumbled.

3. Add some fresh or freeze-dried raspberries to serve, and enjoy!

Tip: Swap raspberries for strawberries if you prefer!

Tropical Smoothie

We are obsessed with this in summer! It is like a holiday in a glass - I'm not even kidding. Put it in a tall glass and decorate with a little umbrella if you want to be fancy! Also, to the adults out there... this smoothie works so well with a shot of good quality vodka in it!

PREP TIME: 5 MINUTES | SERVES 2

Ingredients

240ml of coconut water or orange juice

140g frozen mango

140g frozen pineapple

1 ripe banana

1 tsp honey

Method

1. Add your liquid of choice to the blender first, followed by the rest of the ingredients. Blend until really smooth. (We use frozen fruit because it creates such a smooth, creamy consistency when blended.)

2. Pour into a glass and serve! If you like, go fancy and decorate with fresh fruit or a paper umbrella.

Strawberries & Cream Cheesecake

Strawberries and cream are a classic British combo! This smooth and creamy no-bake recipe is so easy to make and the perfect way to celebrate spring and summer. This cheesecake is so delicious because we use fresh strawberries, and they honestly make all the difference in this light and airy dessert!

PREP TIME: 15 MINUTES, PLUS 4 HOURS CHILLING | SERVES 8

Ingredients

175g digestive biscuits

90g butter, melted

250ml double cream

235g cream cheese

1 tsp vanilla extract

120g icing sugar

100g fresh strawberries

Method

1. Place the digestive biscuits into a sandwich bag and use a rolling pin to crush them. Alternatively, use a food processor and blitz to a fine crumb.

2. Add the biscuit crumb and melted butter to a bowl and mix until fully combined.

3. Line and grease an 8-inch cake tin then add the biscuit mix to the tin. Firmly press the biscuit mix down into the bottom of the tin until it forms an even base.

4. In a separate bowl, whisk the cream until it forms stiff peaks, but be careful not to overmix it or it'll look like scrambled eggs!

5. In another bowl, whisk the cream cheese, vanilla and icing sugar together.

6. In a third bowl, use a fork to roughly squash the strawberries until they become a purée, but leave a few larger bits in for texture.

7. Combine the strawberries with the cream cheese mixture, then gently fold in the whipped cream.

8. Add the cheesecake filling to the tin and smooth it out evenly, then chill in the fridge for up to 4 hours to set.

9. Slice and enjoy!

Tip: We also like to pipe a little whipped cream on top and decorate it with a few fresh strawberries.

Blueberry & Lemon Cookies

Now this recipe is one of my favourites of the whole book! It isn't one of the typical flavours we sell in store as our chocolate and biscuit flavours are always the most popular, but if you are looking for a lighter, fruitier option, then these are PERFECT! I'm such a blueberry fan anyway, but the lemon just makes these cookies unreal.

PREP TIME: 15 MINUTES | COOKING TIME: 15 MINUTES | MAKES 10

Ingredients

160g caster sugar

1 ½ lemons, zested

120g butter, softened

1 large egg, plus 1 egg yolk

1 tsp vanilla extract

½ tsp baking powder

360g plain flour

2 tsp cornflour

200g white chocolate, cut into chunks

150g fresh blueberries

50g blueberry jam

Method

1. Preheat the oven to 180°c and line three large baking trays.

2. Combine the sugar and lemon zest in a bowl then add the butter, eggs and vanilla, and mix again.

3. Sift in the baking powder, flour and cornflour and fold in the dry ingredients until fully combined. The mixture should start to resemble a dough at this point.

4. Carefully fold in the chocolate, followed by the blueberries, but be careful not to burst any of them!

5. Place a few dollops of blueberry jam over the dough and swirl it through to create a gentle ripple.

6. Divide the dough into ten equal portions and roll into cookie balls. Transfer to the baking trays, allowing plenty of room around each as they will spread while they bake.

7. Bake for 12 to 15 minutes or until golden brown.

8. Allow to cool first then enjoy (or maybe just have a nibble as it's cooling down, because there's nothing better than a freshly baked cookie!).

Tip: Raspberry jam works just as well in this recipe if you don't have blueberry jam.

Lemonade Cooler

Tart, sweet and refreshing. This reminds me of the lemonade you get in America
– it's the perfect easy drink for a hot summer's day, or any day really!

PREP TIME: 25 MINUTES | COOKING TIME: 5 MINUTES | SERVES 5

Ingredients

6 lemons

150g caster sugar

1.25L still water

A handful of fresh mint leaves, to taste

250ml soda water

Ice, to serve

Method

1. Squeeze the juice of two lemons into a saucepan, then place the squeezed lemon halves into the pan too.

2. Add the sugar, 250ml of still water, and a few sprigs of mint (to taste) to the pan. Bring to the boil until the sugar is fully dissolved.

3. Add more mint leaves or sugar, depending on how you like your lemonade, then when you're happy with the taste and everything is combined, take off the heat, cover, and set aside for 20 minutes.

4. Strain into a large serving jug and pour in the remaining water and soda water.

5. Add the juice of the remaining lemons and stir, but be careful not to add the pips!

6. Pour the lemonade into a glass over ice, garnish with mint leaves, and enjoy!

Tip: We like to add frozen raspberries for an extra little something, too!

Dol

DESSERTS
OPEN
Dolly's

Chocolate Orange Brownies

Rich chocolate and zesty orange have been a match made in heaven for, like, forever. My nan gets me a chocolate orange every year, so these brownies are a must for us during that random period between Christmas and New Year when no one knows what day it is. All I'm gonna say is... warm? With ice cream? Perfection.

PREP TIME: 10 MINUTES | COOKING TIME: 25 MINUTES | MAKES 9

Ingredients

180g caster sugar

95g light soft brown sugar

185g salted butter, melted

3 eggs

1 tsp orange essence

50g cocoa powder

100g plain flour

200g good quality dark chocolate

4 x 90g chocolate orange bars

Chocolate orange segments, to decorate

Method

1. Preheat the oven 180°c and grease and line your 20x20cm baking tin.

2. In a large bowl, using a mixer or handheld whisk, mix the sugars and butter together..

3. Add the eggs and orange essence and mix until fully combined.

4. Add the cocoa powder carefully, making sure it's mixed evenly throughout the batter.

5. Gradually sift in the flour and mix well.

6. Melt the chocolate in 20-second bursts in a microwave, then fold it through the batter.

7. Place half the batter into the baking tin and spread it out evenly to the edges.

8. Top with the chocolate orange bars and spread the rest of the batter on the top, ensuring none of the chocolate bars can be seen.

9. Bake in the oven for 20 to 25 minutes - a smooth, shiny film on top is a good indication of the perfect brownie!

10. Remove from the oven and immediately place a segment of chocolate orange on what will be the top of each portion. Basically, it will melt onto each slice and then set once it's been in the fridge.

11. Once cooled to room temperature, place the brownie in the fridge for a minimum of 6 hours, but preferably overnight.

12. Slice into your desired portions and you're done! Perfection.

Lemon Pie Blondies

These are the definition of bittersweet! The tart lemon combined with the buttery cookie takes this blondie to the next level. This fudgy traybake is so easy to throw together and will last up to 10 days in the fridge, so you can keep going back for a nibble!

PREP TIME: 10 MINUTES | COOKING TIME: 30 MINUTES | MAKES 9

Ingredients

150g salted butter, melted

180g caster sugar

3 eggs

1 tsp vanilla extract

270g plain flour

200g white chocolate chips

3 tbsp Cookie Crumb (see page 189)

270g lemon curd

Method

1. Preheat the oven to 180°c and line a 20x20cm baking tray with greaseproof paper..

2. Cream the melted butter and sugar together in a bowl, then add the eggs and vanilla extract before mixing again.

3. Sift in the flour and fold until combined.

4. Melt the white chocolate chips, add them to the bowl, and mix until combined. (Make sure the chocolate isn't too hot though as you don't want to start cooking the eggs too early.)

5. Add half the batter to the tray and smooth it out to the edges.

6. Sprinkle 2 tablespoons of Cookie Crumb onto the batter, then add the remaining batter and spread it out to the edges again.

7. Add the lemon curd to a piping bag (or sandwich bag if you don't have one) and pipe the lemon curd onto the blondie batter in diagonal lines. Drag a sharp knife through the lines in the opposite direction to create a feathered pattern.

8. Sprinkle the remaining Cookie Crumb on top and tap the tray on a work surface to remove any air bubbles.

9. Bake for 25 to 30 minutes. (When it comes out of the oven, the centre may still be a little jiggly, this is totally normal!)

10. Allow to cool to room temperature, then pop in the fridge overnight. (I know, I know, you just want to eat them straight away, but trust me - the blondies need to be set properly before you chop into them!)

11. Once you have been so patient, slice them up and enjoy!

Tip: Switch out the Cookie Crumb for crumbled meringue if you fancy! You can also pop a slice into the microwave for a few seconds and serve it with some cream or ice cream for the most unreal pudding!

Luxury Dipped Strawberries

We first started selling these in lockdown and they were such a hit! They are so easy and look so effective if you're making an inexpensive gift for someone. Fresh, juicy strawberries dipped in rich chocolate are the perfect combination!

PREP TIME: 10 MINUTES , PLUS 1 HOUR CHILLING | COOKING TIME: 5 MINUTES | MAKES 12

Ingredients

12 fresh large strawberries (with strong stalks)

250g good quality milk chocolate

250g good quality white chocolate

Method

1. Line a large board or tray with greaseproof paper. (We wouldn't recommend a plate as you want a perfectly flat surface.)

2. Thoroughly wash the strawberries and dry with a paper towel.

3. Melt the milk and white chocolate in two separate bowls. You can do this over a pot of hot water, or just pop them in the microwave in 20-second bursts!

4. Transfer the melted chocolate into two narrow, deep containers, like a tall glass or a small jug - you want to be able to coat the strawberries in one dip, so don't use a shallow bowl (like I did when I first tried this - it didn't look cute).

5. Carefully pick up a washed strawberry by its stalk and dip it into the milk chocolate, making small circular motions to cover all the fruit.

6. Once the strawberry is fully coated, lift it out of the glass and wiggle it slightly so any excess chocolate drips off.

7. Gently scrape one side of the strawberry on the edge of the glass or container (whichever side will come into contact with the tray) and place it on the greaseproof paper. This creates a flatter surface and stops the chocolate spreading out too much.

8. Repeat this with five more strawberries to make six in total, then repeat steps 5 to 8 with the white chocolate and remaining strawberries.

9. Transfer the leftover white and milk chocolate to two piping bags. Handling them one at a time, cut a small hole in the piping bag and drizzle each strawberry carefully and quickly. (I like to drizzle milk chocolate ones with white chocolate and vice versa, but you can do whichever way you fancy!)

10. Place the dipped strawberries in the fridge for 1 hour to cool and harden.

11. Once the chocolate strawberries have set, arrange them however you like! You can pop each one in a bun case and place it in a fancy box for a gift, or you can arrange them on a board and serve!

Banana Sushi

Being TikTok girlies, you knew we couldn't miss out on some viral desserts, and this is one of them! This is such a fun one to make as you really can let your imagination run wild. Switch out almost any of the spreads and toppings to suit you!

PREP TIME: 15 MINUTES | COOKING TIME: 10 MINUTES | MAKES 6

Ingredients

FOR THE CREPES

125g plain flour

Pinch of salt

250ml milk

1 large egg

FOR THE FILLINGS AND TOPPINGS (SUGGESTED)

Bananas

Nutella

Peanut butter

White chocolate spread

Strawberries

Chopped nuts

Method

FOR THE CREPES

1. In a bowl, whisk the flour, salt and milk together.

2. Add the egg and whisk again until fully combined (make sure there are no lumps!).

3. Put a medium-sized non-stick frying pan on a medium heat and add a little bit of butter (honestly, you don't need a lot as you don't want the crepes to be greasy!).

4. Pour a bit of the batter into the pan and swirl it around until the bottom of the pan is coated in the batter. You want a nice thin crepe.

5. Once the crepe has formed in the pan, leave it to cook for a minute, then flip! (You can flip it like it's pancake day if you want, but if you wanna play it safe, just use a rubber spatula to flip.)

6. Once you have a nice colour on your crepe, pop it on a plate and set it aside, then repeat the process with the rest of the batter. It will make around six crepes.

FOR THE ASSEMBLY

7. Assembly time! This is where it has to look pretty. Use the same fillings for all your sushi pieces or mix and match. It's completely up to you!

8. Spread a thin layer of Nutella over a crepe and place your peeled banana to the edge. Now, roll it up.

9. Repeat this with white chocolate spread, peanut butter, caramel - any combo you fancy!

10. Once you have your little crepe rolls, you can go a bit fancy and top them with some more spread, sliced strawberries, nuts, and any other toppings you like.

11. Slice the crepes into sushi rolls and display on a board or plate. Now it's time to eat... and you can't eat sushi without chopsticks!

Tilly's Mini Pavlovas

Hi, Tilly here! I've been a baker at Dolly's since October 2023. I'm constantly laughing and chatting while at work and I love making all the bakes we sell, but my all-time favourite is my mini pavlovas! They're the first things I learnt to make in my baking career and I've loved them ever since. I hope you do, too!

PREP TIME: 20 MINUTES | COOKING TIME: 1 HOUR, PLUS 25 MINUTES RESTING IN THE OVEN | SERVES 8

Ingredients

4 eggs whites

Caster sugar (twice the weight of the egg whites)

225ml double cream

Fruit of your choice, like strawberries, raspberries or blueberries

Dusting of icing sugar, to serve

Method

1. Preheat the oven to 110ºc and line a large baking tray with greaseproof paper.
2. Weigh out the egg whites and times this weight by two to figure out the amount of caster sugar you'll need.
3. In a large glass bowl, beat the egg whites on a fast speed using an electric whisk until stiff peaks form.
4. Gradually add the sugar, gently folding with a metal spoon until snow white and glossy.
5. Flip the bowl upside down to check the mixture - it shouldn't budge! (If you don't do this above your head then did you really test it?)
6. Place the mixture into a large piping bag with a wide nozzle and pipe circles, 10cm in diameter, onto the greaseproof paper, leaving a slight hollow in the middle and a space between each pavlova nest. You can use the back of a spoon to help smooth and shape them.
7. Bake for 1 hour, then turn the oven off but leave the meringues inside for a further 25 minutes.
8. Once the meringues have cooled, you can start whipping the cream. In a separate bowl, whip the double cream until it forms soft peaks. Remove the meringues from the oven and allow to cool to room temperature.
9. Scoop the cream into each nest and top with sliced fruit in whatever pattern you like!
10. Dust with icing sugar to serve.

Tip: Don't worry if you over-whip the cream - this can be sorted by adding a splash more cream and folding it in with a spatula.

Banoffee Pie Pancake Stack

A staple item that has been on our menu from the very beginning! Soft, fluffy pancakes, fresh banana, and sticky caramel, finished with a cookie crumb. An elite combo in our opinion.

PREP TIME: 10 MINUTES | COOKING TIME: 10 MINUTES | SERVES 2

Ingredients

75g butter, melted

50g granulated sugar

2 eggs

350ml milk

1 tsp vanilla extract

1 tsp salt

300g plain flour

2 tsp baking powder

2 bananas, sliced

Cookie Crumb (approximately 100g, but you can follow your heart! See page 189)

Caramel Spread (approximately 100g, see page 187)

Whipped cream, to serve

Method

1. Add the melted butter, sugar, eggs, milk, vanilla and salt to a bowl, then whisk until combined.
2. Slowly sift in the flour and baking powder and mix to form a batter.
3. Heat a large pan on a medium heat.
4. Add an extra knob of butter to stop the pancakes from sticking, then carefully spoon the batter into the pan to make small 3-inch pancakes. (Depending on the size of your pan, you might have to do this a few times until you have used all the batter.)
5. Once air bubbles start to form on the pancakes, it's time to flip them. Using a spatula, carefully flip over each pancake and cook for another 2 to 3 minutes.
6. Transfer the pancakes onto a plate so you're ready to start stacking!
7. Starting with one pancake, add a teaspoon of Caramel Spread, some sliced banana and a teaspoon of Cookie Crumb, then add the next pancake and repeat. Each stack should be around four pancakes in our opinion.
8. Top with more Caramel Spread, sliced banana and Cookie Crumb, then finish with whipped cream and enjoy!

Tip: This is so good if you have leftover Caramel Spread, but it can also be switched for Dolly's Caramel Sauce, or any sauce for that matter. Add white chocolate buttons if you're not a fan of bananas - the caramel and white chocolate combo really works!

Strawberry Shortcake Freakshake

Nothing has the "wow" factor quite like a freakshake! There's really no right or wrong way to make one of thee - just let your imagination run wild.

PREP TIME: 10 MINUTES | SERVES 2

Ingredients

FOR THE SHAKE

6 scoops Strawberry Ice Cream (see page 170)

1 handful of frozen strawberries

250ml full fat milk

TO DECORATE

White Chocolate Spread (see page 188)

2 digestive biscuits, crushed

White chocolate chips

Sprinkle (of your choice)

2 slices Strawberries and Cream Cheesecake (see page 28)

Dolly's White Chocolate Sauce

Whipped cream

8 fresh strawberries, stalks removed

8 large marshmallows

Method

1. Grab two tall, fancy glasses that are able to support the cheesecake slice.

2. Paint a thick layer of white chocolate spread on the rim of each glass using a spatula.

3. Crush the digestive biscuits and roll each glass in the crumbs so they stick to the spread.

4. Stick on the chocolate chips and sprinkles in a design of your choice.

5. Take the white chocolate sauce and place little drips around the top of the glass, allowing it to drip down the inside of the glass at different levels, then set aside.

6. Next, place all the shake ingredients into a blender and mix until it combines and forms a thick, smooth paste.

7. Pour the shake into the glasses and quickly place the slices of cheesecake on the top.

8. Fill in the gaps around the base of the cheesecake with fresh whipped cream.

9. Place four strawberries and four marshmallows onto a skewer, snap it to the size of your glass, and then place it inside the freakshake. Repeat for the second glass and serve immediately.

Tip: You can honestly adapt this however you wish. Swap out the chocolate chips and strawberries for sweets and the cheesecake for a slice of cake or a doughnut.

Iced Blueberry Matcha Latte

Matcha is the new "It girl" when it comes to drinks, but not everyone knows how easy it is to make! We have absolutely mastered our Iced Blueberry Matcha Latte recipe, and it's the perfect combo of sweet, creamy, and refreshing!

PREP TIME: 10 MINUTES | COOKING TIME: 15 MINUTES | SERVES 2

Ingredients

FOR THE BLUEBERRY SYRUP

125g fresh blueberries

125g water

125g sugar

FOR THE MATCHA LATTE

400ml milk (whichever you prefer)

2 tsp matcha powder

Ice, to serve

Method

FOR THE BLUEBERRY SYRUP

1. Add the blueberries, water and sugar to a small saucepan.

2. Stir over a medium heat for 10 minutes until it begins to bubble

3. Turn down to low and simmer until all the blueberries have reduced and the mixture becomes syrupy.

4. Remove from the heat, allow to cool for a few minutes, then transfer to a sterilised jar or container. (This can be kept in the fridge for up to 2 weeks.)

FOR THE MATCHA LATTE

5. Add 3 tablespoons of blueberry syrup to a glass with a splash of milk and whisk until fully combined.

6. Fill the glass with ice, then add 200ml of milk. (If you have a slightly smaller glass, you might want to use less – just make sure you leave a little bit of room at the top to add your matcha.)

7. Spoon 1 teaspoon of matcha powder into a small bowl and add a splash of water.

8. Whisk for 1 minute until the matcha becomes frothy.

9. Pour the matcha over the milk, then repeat the steps for the second glass.

10. You should have three beautiful, colourful layers. Add a straw, stir and enjoy!

Dolly's
DESSERTS
Dolly's
DESSERT

Chocoholic

Let's talk chocolate. This is the most rich and indulgent section of the book, and it is perfect for anyone who is a real-life chocoholic. From our iconic stuffed cookies to our OG Chocolate Brownies, we're sure this chapter will be a firm favourite of yours.

Triple Chocolate Stuffed Cookies

There is a reason these 3 types of chocolate exist, and we're convinced it's so they can go in this recipe. That's how nice it is. These chocolate overload cookies are a real show stopper, and one of these served warm with a scoop of ice cream is absolutely unbeatable.

PREP TIME: 15 MINUTES, PLUS 3 HOURS FREEZING | COOKING TIME: 15 MINUTES | MAKES 6

Ingredients

115g butter, softened

160g light soft brown sugar

40g caster sugar

1 large egg

1 tbsp milk

2 tsp vanilla extract

280g plain flour

1 tsp baking powder

80g cocoa powder

1 tsp bicarbonate of soda

75g milk chocolate chips

75g white chocolate chips

75g dark chocolate chips

170g white chocolate

Method

1. In a bowl, whisk the softened butter, light soft brown sugar and caster sugar together until soft and fluffy.

2. Add the egg, milk and the vanilla, and whisk again until combined.

3. Sift in the flour, baking powder, cocoa powder and bicarb, then mix with a spatula or cookie rod to form a dough.

4. Add the milk, white and dark chocolate chips to the dough and mix to combine.

5. Place the dough onto a worktop or board and cut into six equal portions. Roll each section into a ball then flatten it out.

6. Break up the white chocolate into squares and divide it between the cookie dough, adding a few squares into the middle of each cookie.

7. Wrap the dough around the chocolate and roll it into balls again. You should be left with six stuffed cookie dough balls.

8. Place them onto a lined baking tray and freeze for at least 3 hours.

9. Bake for 12 to 14 minutes in a preheated oven at 180ºc.

10. Allow to cool and enjoy! (To be fair, you don't even have to wait as these can be eaten while slightly warm and all gooey inside.)

Tip: If it's Christmas, these are the absolute BEST IDEA! If you top the cookies with some melted white chocolate and holly leaves, they look just like little Christmas puddings!

Cadbury's Caramel Brookies

These are absolutely stunning. We are obsessed with the combination of rich, gooey brownie, chewy cookie, and Cadbury's caramel stuffing. Perfection. There's no way anyone can say no to one of these bad boys.

PREP TIME: 25 MINUTES | COOKING TIME: 25 MINUTES | MAKES 9

Ingredients

FOR THE COOKIE LAYER

115g caster sugar

225g plain flour

¼ tsp baking powder

¼ tsp bicarbonate of soda

150g salted butter, softened

1 egg, plus 1 egg yolk

300g milk chocolate chips

425g Cadbury's Caramel

FOR THE BROWNIE LAYER

140g caster sugar

70g light soft brown sugar

140g salted butter, melted

2 large eggs

40g cocoa powder

80g plain flour

150g dark chocolate

1 tsp vanilla extract

Method

1. Grease and line a 20x20cm baking tin and preheat the oven 180°c.
2. For the cookie layer, start by mixing caster sugar, plain flour, baking powder and bicarbonate of soda together in a large bowl.
3. Add the softened butter, egg, and egg yolk to the bowl and mix again. Tip in the chocolate chips and stir to combine.
4. Once fully combined, add to the baking tray and spread out evenly to create the first layer.
5. Add the Cadbury's Caramel bars to create the second layer, covering the whole base and leaving no gaps. Set the tray to one side while you make the brownie batter.
6. For the brownie, start by mixing the caster sugar, soft brown sugar and butter in a bowl (you can wash the bowl you just used if you want to minimise the washing up!).
7. Add the eggs and mix until fully combined.
8. Add the cocoa powder carefully, making sure it's mixed evenly throughout.
9. Gradually sift in the flour and mix well. Melt the chocolate in 20-second bursts in a microwave, then fold it through the batter along with the vanilla extract.
10. Pour the brownie batter over the top of the caramel bars to create the third layer, making sure to spread it right to the edges.
11. Bake for 20 to 25 minutes. The brownie layer should have a shiny coating on top! That's how you know you have got it perfect!
12. Once cooled, refrigerate for at least 5 hours or overnight (I know this is annoying, we get impatient too, but honestly it will be worth it to make sure it's set.)
13. Slice into nine portions and serve. These will keep in an airtight container in the fridge for 10 days.

No-bake Mars Bar Slice

This no-bake recipe is quick and easy to follow and it's so, so delicious. If you're a last-minuter like us, this is great to throw together and it looks impressive, too. It's buttery, gooey and perfect with a cup of tea!

PREP TIME: 15 MINUTES, PLUS 4 HOURS CHILLING | MAKES 8

Ingredients

350g digestive biscuits

125g salted butter, melted

1 x 397g tin of condensed milk

8 large Mars bars

300g milk chocolate

Method

1. Crush the digestive biscuits into a fine crumb. You can do this by using a food processor, but if you don't have one, a sealable sandwich bag and a rolling pin are your best friends.
2. Pour the biscuit crumbs and 100g of the melted butter into a bowl and mix well.
3. Add the condensed milk and mix the ingredients together until fully combined.
4. Cut five of the Mars bars into chunks (whichever size you like) and fold them into the base mix.
5. Place the mixture into a lined and greased baking tin, approx. 20x20cm.
6. Press down evenly and firmly using the back of a spoon to cover the whole tray.
7. Pop the chocolate and remaining 25g of butter into a microwaveable bowl. Melt in 20-second bursts until silky and smooth, but be careful not to burn it.
8. Pour the chocolate over the top of the base, then chop the remaining Mars bars into thin slices and use them to decorate however you fancy.
9. Refrigerate for 4 hours, then chop into 8 portions and serve. These can be kept in an airtight container in the fridge for 1 to 2 weeks.

Tip: You can substitute the Mars bars for a Snickers, Boost, Milky Way or whatever your favourite bar is.

Bueno & Nutella Brownies

This is the OG recipe that always sells out first. Nothing looks more impressive than when you cut these open and see the Bueno in the middle. Everyone is Bueno MAD. We always say stick a Bueno on anything and it will sell. The hype is real but definitely not overrated. Gooey, fudgy and with Nutella in it too… UNREAL!

PREP TIME: 10 MINUTES, PLUS 8 HOURS CHILLING | COOKING TIME: 25 MINUTES | MAKES 9

Ingredients

90g light soft brown sugar

180g caster sugar

185g salted butter, melted

3 eggs

1 tsp vanilla extract

50g cocoa powder

100g plain flour

200g good quality dark chocolate

6 Kinder Bueno bars (12 sticks of Bueno in total)

300g Nutella

Method

1. Preheat the oven to 180ºc and grease and line a 20x20cm baking tin.
2. In a large bowl, using a mixer or handheld whisk, mix both of the sugars and the melted butter together until creamy.
3. Add the eggs and vanilla extract and mix until fully combined.
4. Add the cocoa powder carefully, making sure it's mixed evenly throughout.
5. Gradually sift in the flour and mix well until you can no longer see any remaining.
6. Melt the chocolate in 20-second bursts in a microwave, then pour into the batter and fold it through.
7. Place half the batter into the baking tin and spread it evenly around the tray.
8. Place the unwrapped Buenos on top of the batter, making sure to cover the whole tray if you want the full effect.
9. Spread a thick layer of Nutella over the top of the Buenos, then pour the remaining brownie batter over the top. Make sure all the Buenos are completely covered to prevent the wafers from burning.
10. Bake for 25 minutes. It should have a shiny layer on the top and be slightly jiggly in the middle when it comes out. If you've got that, you've done it totally right!
11. Allow to cool slightly, then place the brownie tray in the fridge for at least 8 hours. (Overnight is best, if we're honest. I know you wanna eat them now but trust me on this!)
12. Remove from the tin and use a sharp knife to cut into nine or whatever portion sizes you like. Store in a cool place in an airtight container for up to a week

Tip: Wipe your knife after every slice to get a super clean cut!

Cookies & Cream Brookie

Brookies have grown so much in popularity over the years and I can see why! They are half gooey, fudgy brownie and half buttery, doughy cookie. Although these are pretty impressive as is, we obviously had to take these to the next level by adding a cookies and cream layer to the middle.

PREP TIME: 25 MINUTES | COOKING TIME: 25 MINUTES | MAKES 12

Ingredients

FOR THE COOKIE LAYER

115g caster sugar

115g light soft brown sugar

135g unsalted butter, room temperature

1 egg, plus 1 egg yolk

225g plain flour

60g cocoa powder

½ tsp bicarbonate of soda

¼ tsp baking powder

200g white chocolate chips

200g milk chocolate chips

FOR THE COOKIES AND CREAM FILLING

2 packets of Oreos or cookies and cream biscuits (about 300g)

1 full jar cookies and cream spread or 500g White Chocolate Spread (see page 188)

FOR THE BROWNIE LAYER

140g caster sugar

70g light soft brown sugar

140g salted butter, melted

2 large eggs

40g cocoa powder

75g plain flour

150g good quality dark chocolate

1 tsp vanilla extract

Method

1. Preheat the oven 180°c and grease and line a 20x20cm baking tin.

2. Starting with the cookie layer, add the caster sugar, light brown sugar and butter to a bowl and cream together. Add the egg and yolk and mix again.

3. Sift in the plain flour, cocoa powder, bicarbonate of soda and baking powder, then mix until combined.

4. Add the chocolate chips and mix again (you can do this with your hands as it should now resemble a workable dough).

5. Place the cookie dough into the tray and spread it out evenly to create the first layer.

6. Cover the cookie layer with Oreos or any cookies and cream cookies you can get your hands on!

7. Pop the jar of cookies and cream spread in the microwave for a few seconds (this slightly melts it, making it easier to spread.)

8. Pour the melty spread over the cookies and spread it around evenly with a spatula. Cover with cling film and set this aside while you make the brownie batter.

9. To make the brownie layer, start by mixing the sugars and the melted butter together in a large bowl with an electric or handheld whisk. Add the eggs and mix until fully combined.

10. Add the cocoa powder carefully, making sure it's mixed evenly throughout. Gradually sift in the flour and mix well.

11. Melt the dark chocolate in 20-second bursts in a microwave then fold it through the batter.

12. Pour the brownie batter evenly on top of the other layers in the tray, then pop it in the oven and bake for 20 to 25 minutes. The brownie layer should have a shiny film on the top while baking.

13. Once it's done, set it aside to cool (it may look slightly jiggly in the centre, but this is normal!).

14. Place in the fridge to set for around 6 hours or preferably overnight. Cut into 12 portions and enjoy!

Nutella Chocolate French Toast

Gooey in the middle, this is a chocoholic's absolute dream breakfast, brunch or midnight snack. This recipe is so versatile - try using different bread and chocolate combos for a new taste every time! Drizzle with your favourite syrup and serve with some fresh fruit if you're feeling a bit fancy!

PREP TIME: 5 MINUTES | COOKING TIME: 10 MINUTES | SERVES 2

Ingredients

2 eggs

2 tbsp milk

1 tsp vanilla extract

4 slices of bread (we like a fresh white bloomer)

4 tbsp Nutella

1 tbsp ground cinnamon

6 tbsp granulated sugar

Dusting of icing sugar, to serve

Method

1. In a large, flat dish (big enough for the slices of bread) whisk the eggs, milk and vanilla together.

2. Create 2 Nutella sandwiches, using 2 tablespoons of Nutella in each one.

3. On a plate, combine the cinnamon and granulated sugar and set aside.

4. Grease a large frying pan with a little butter and pop it on a medium heat.

5. Place each sandwich in the egg wash, coating it on all sides, then fry on each side until crisp and golden.

6. Hot from the pan, pop the French toast into the cinnamon sugar mix and coat generously.

7. Once fully coated, plate up with a dusting of icing sugar and enjoy!

Triple Chocolate Pancake Stack

Breakfast doesn't get any more indulgent than this! These fluffy chocolate pancakes are guaranteed to satisfy any sweet tooth and will definitely get you out of bed in the morning!

PREP TIME: 5 MINUTES | COOKING TIME: 10 MINUTES | SERVES 4

Ingredients

75g butter, melted

50g granulated sugar

2 eggs

350ml milk

1 tsp vanilla extract

300g plain flour

50g cocoa powder

2 tsp baking powder

1 tsp salt

40g white chocolate chips

40g milk chocolate chips

Chocolate sauce or spread (we use our Dolly's Milk Chocolate Dessert Sauce)

Method

1. Add the melted butter, sugar, eggs, milk, and vanilla to a bowl and whisk to combine.

2. Slowly sift in the flour, cocoa powder, baking powder, and salt, then mix again.

3. Once the batter has formed, fold in the chocolate chips.

4. Heat a large pan on a medium heat and add a little butter to stop the pancakes from sticking.

5. Carefully spoon the batter into the pan to make small 3-inch pancakes. (Depending on the size of your pan, you might have to do this a few times until you have used all the batter.)

6. Once air bubbles start to form on the top of the pancakes, it's time to flip. Use a spatula to carefully flip each pancake and cook them for another 2 to 3 minutes on the other side.

7. Transfer the pancakes to a plate 'cause it's time to start stacking!

8. Start with one pancake and add a layer of chocolate sauce or spread. Add another pancake on top and repeat. Each stack should be around four pancakes tall (in our opinion).

9. Top with some more chocolatey sauce and maybe a few more chocolate chips. To finish, we like to add cream or a big scoop of ice cream!

Stuffed Nutella Pancakes

This is an absolute favourite with our customers and a combo that will never ever get old. Nutella and pancakes? Erm, yes, please.

PREP TIME: 5 MINUTES | COOKING TIME: 15 MINUTES | SERVES 4

Ingredients

75g butter, melted

50g granulated sugar

2 eggs

350ml milk

1 tsp vanilla extract

300g plain flour

1 tsp salt

2 tsp baking powder

12 tsp Nutella (approx. 1 tsp per pancake)

Dusting of icing sugar, to serve

Method

1. Add the melted butter, sugar, eggs, milk, vanilla to a bowl and whisk until combined.

2. Slowly sift in the flour, salt, and baking powder, then mix until the batter has formed.

3. Heat a large frying pan on a medium heat and melt a little butter to stop the pancakes from sticking. Carefully spoon the batter into the pan to make small 3-inch pancakes.

4. Spoon 1 teaspoon of Nutella into the centre of each pancake and then cover with a teaspoon of pancake batter to "stuff" the pancakes. (Depending on the size of your pan, you might have to do this a few times until you have used up all the batter.)

5. Once air bubbles start to form on top of the pancakes, it's time to flip them. Use a spatula to carefully flip each pancake and then cook them for another 2 to 3 minutes on the other side.

6. Transfer the pancakes onto a plate and dust with a little icing sugar to decorate!

7. We like to have these with strawberries and whipped cream, but serve them as you please and enjoy!

Honeycomb Rocky Road

Crunchy honeycomb, soft marshmallow and buttery biscuit… What a combination of textures and flavour! It's so easy to make and there's absolutely no baking involved! Swap out the Crunchie bars for Twixes if you want a more soft and chewy treat.

PREP TIME: 15 MINUTES, PLUS 3 HOURS CHILLING | MAKES 12

Ingredients

125g salted butter, melted

300g milk chocolate, roughly chopped

100g dark chocolate, roughly chopped

125g golden syrup

180g digestive biscuits

6 large Crunchie bars

100g mini marshmallows

Method

1. Line and grease a 20x20cm baking tin.
2. In a large mixing bowl, add the melted butter, chocolate chunks and golden syrup.
3. Give this a really good mix until all the chocolate is melted and combined. If it needs a little extra heat to melt it, pop the bowl in the microwave and heat for 20 seconds.
4. Break the digestive biscuits into bite-sized pieces (not crumbs) and roughly chop the Crunchies.
5. Add the mini marshmallows, Crunchie pieces and digestive pieces to the mix and stir until completely covered in the melted chocolate mixture.
6. Tip into the baking tin and smooth out to the edges, then place in the fridge for at least 3 hours to set.
7. Chop into portions and store in an airtight container for 2 to 3 weeks.

Tip: Run the knife under hot water after each chop to ensure you get perfectly neat slices!

The OG Chocolate Brownie

You can't beat the originals, and this is our unbeatable chocolate brownie recipe. My mum worked tirelessly in the kitchen for years to perfect this recipe and she's really cracked it! These are the fudgiest, richest and most chocolatey brownies. It's everything you could ever want in a brownie.

PREP TIME: 10 MINUTES, PLUS 4 HOURS CHILLING | COOKING TIME: 25 MINUTES | MAKES 9

Ingredients

180g caster sugar

95g light soft brown sugar

185g salted butter, softened

3 eggs

1 tsp vanilla extract

60g cocoa powder

100g plain flour

200g good quality dark chocolate

150g milk chocolate chunks

150g white chocolate chunks

Method

1. Preheat the oven to 180°c and line and grease a 20x20cm baking tin.

2. In a large bowl, using a mixer or handheld whisk, cream the sugars and butter together.

3. Add the eggs and vanilla extract, then mix again until combined.

4. Sift in the cocoa powder and stir, making sure it's mixed evenly throughout.

5. Gradually sift in the flour and mix until fully incorporated.

6. Melt the dark chocolate in 20-second bursts in a microwave and add it to the batter. (Yes, dark chocolate! It's not everyone's favourite, but trust me when I say no brownie is worth eating if it's not made using dark chocolate. It makes the most gooey and rich brownie.)

7. Mix in the milk chocolate and white chocolate chunks, then pour the batter into the baking tin and bake for 20 to 25 minutes. Once baked, there should be a glossy coating on top of the brownie (this is how you know you've got it perfect!)

8. Allow to cool, then refrigerate for at least 4 hours or preferably overnight. (I know, I know. It's a long time and you just wanna dig in straight away, but trust me, it's worth the wait as you don't want sloppy brownies!)

9. Slice into nine portions and enjoy!

Tip: For the most luxurious dessert, reheat a slice in the microwave for 20 seconds and serve with our Vanilla Ice Cream (see page 176) and a bit of Dolly's sauce drizzled over the top!

Chocolate Lava Cake

This recipe is honestly so impressive that nobody would ever know just how easy
it is to make! It's pure chocolate heaven and couldn't be left out of a chapter
called "Chocoholic". This screams indulgence and will go down an absolute
treat after a Sunday dinner with some ice cream!

PREP TIME: 10 MINUTES | COOKING TIME: 15 MINUTES | SERVES 6

Ingredients

120g unsalted butter, plus 10g for greasing

180g good quality dark chocolate

40g caster sugar

2 eggs, plus 2 yolks

3 tbsp plain flour

20g cocoa powder

Pinch of salt

Dusting of icing sugar, to serve

Method

1. Preheat the oven to 220°c and generously grease six ramekins with butter. Cut some greaseproof paper to fit into the bottom of each ramekin and place it neatly into the bottom of each one.

2. Roughly chop the dark chocolate and place it into a large heatproof bowl with the remaining butter. Place the bowl over a pan of boiling water and stir until melted.

3. Turn the pan off but leave the bowl on top to keep warm.

4. In a separate bowl, mix the caster sugar, eggs and yolks until pale in colour and frothy with loads of air bubbles. This might take a while, but it will get there!

5. Sift in the flour, cocoa powder, and salt, then whisk again until fully combined.

6. Carefully fold the melted chocolate through, a bit at a time, to keep the air in the batter.

7. Fill the ramekins three quarters of the way up with the batter and bake for 10 to 12 minutes.

8. Allow to cool for a couple of minutes, then carefully run a sharp knife around the edge of the ramekin.

9. Turn each ramekin upside down on a small plate to empty out the chocolate cake, then remove the greaseproof paper from the top.

10. Dust with icing sugar and serve immediately with vanilla ice cream, custard, or cream.

Nutty Brownie Bombs

I don't think we need to convince anyone to try these - just look at them! Ferrero Rocher are a staple in our house at Christmas, so these giant versions go down such a treat! The fudgy brownie, crunchy coating, and the truffle filling is just unreal.

PREP TIME: 20 MINUTES, PLUS 9 HOURS CHILLING | COOKING TIME: 25 MINUTES | MAKES 6

Ingredients

FOR THE BROWNIE

140g caster sugar

70g light soft brown sugar

145g salted butter, melted

2 eggs, plus 1 egg yolk

40g cocoa powder

80g plain flour

1 tsp salt

150g dark chocolate

FOR THE BOMBS

200g Nutella

6 Ferrero Rocher chocolates

300g milk chocolate chips

100g hazelnuts, chopped

Method

1. Line and grease a 20x20cm baking tin, and preheat the oven to 180°c.

2. Add the caster sugar, soft brown sugar and melted butter to a mixing bowl and cream together until smooth.

3. Add the eggs and extra egg yolk and stir to combine.

4. Gradually sift in the cocoa powder, flour and salt and fold through until fully combined.

5. Melt the dark chocolate in 20-second bursts in the microwave, then mix the melted chocolate into the batter.

6. Transfer to the baking tin and smooth out so it evenly covers the base, then bake for 18 to 20 minutes.

7. Allow to cool, then refrigerate for at least 8 hours. (I know it's a long time, but trust me, you want the brownie to set properly!)

8. Line a board or baking tray with greaseproof paper. Then, once set, break the brownie up into small pieces. (Personally, I chuck it in a stand mixer to really help break it down.)

9. Add the Nutella to the broken-up brownie pieces and mix until it's soft and shapeable. (It should kind of resemble Play-Doh.)

10. Weigh out six portions of brownie, around 150g each.

11. Unwrap six Ferrero Rocher truffles and encase each one in the brownie mixture to make six brownie bombs.

12. Melt the milk chocolate chips in 20-second bursts in the microwave, then stir in the chopped hazelnuts.

13. Carefully place a brownie bomb in the chocolate and coat fully. Set aside on the lined tray and repeat with each brownie bomb.

14. Refrigerate for another hour and they are done!

Tip: If you want to make these extra special or gift them to someone, wrap them in greaseproof paper and gold foil!

FERRERO
ROCHER
FERRERO
ROCHER

Triple Chocolate Hot Cookie Dough

This is honestly the most indulgent recipe there is! We're not kidding when we say this is a chocoholic's dream. Who doesn't love the contrast of hot, rich cookie dough and cold, creamy ice cream!

PREP TIME: 10 MINUTES | COOKING TIME: 15 MINUTES | SERVES 2

Ingredients

60g salted butter

100g light brown sugar

1 medium egg

1½ tsp vanilla extract

100g plain flour

1 tsp bicarbonate of soda

25g cocoa powder

50g white chocolate, roughly chopped

50g dark chocolat, roughly chopped

50g milk chocolate, roughly chopped

Method

1. Preheat the oven to 160°c.
2. In a mixing bowl, cream together the butter and sugar.
3. Add the egg and vanilla and mix until fully incorporated.
4. Sift in the flour, bicarbonate of soda, cocoa powder, and mix with a hand whisk or spatula until combined.
5. Add all chocolate chunks, combine, then divide the mixture into two oven dishes of your choice.
6. Bake in the oven for 12 to 14 minutes.
7. Remove from the oven and allow to cool for a couple of minutes before serving with vanilla ice cream and Dolly's White and Milk Chocolate Sauces.

Tip: Use good quality chocolate and plain vanilla ice cream so you can really appreciate the full chocolate flavour. Chocolate chips do work but we love to roughly chop a good quality chocolate bar into chunks.

Georga's Cheesecake Brownies

Hi! I'm Georga and I work as a part of the online sales team at Dolly's. I love baking at home, especially brownies and cheesecake, and this recipe is the perfect solution when I just can't decide which to make!
I hope you love making - and eating - them!

PREP TIME: 30 MINUTES, PLUS 6 HOURS CHILLING | COOKING TIME: 40 MINUTES | MAKES 16

Ingredients

FOR THE BROWNIE MIX

185g unsalted butter

200g dark chocolate

3 eggs

185g caster sugar

95g light soft brown sugar

50g cocoa powder

100g plain flour

200g milk chocolate, roughly chopped (or chips)

FOR THE CHEESECAKE

250g full fat cream cheese

100g caster sugar

1 egg

½ tsp vanilla extract

200g white chocolate (optional)

Method

FOR THE BROWNIE BATTER

1. Preheat the oven to 160ºc and line a 20x20cm baking tray with greaseproof paper. Begin by putting a heatproof bowl over a pan of simmering water, then add the dark chocolate and butter and melt together until smooth and combined. Alternativey, melt these ingredients in a microwaveable bowl for 1 minute. Set aside to cool.

2. In a separate bowl, use an electric whisk to mix the eggs and sugars for a few minutes until pale in colour, doubled in size, and mousse-like in texture. To check if it's done, lift out the whisk - the mix should leave behind a trail on the surface of the mixture.

3. Pour the cooled chocolate mix over the sugar and egg mix. Carefully fold until combined (don't rush as it's important to keep the air in!)

4. Sift in the cocoa powder and flour and fold gently to combine before folding through the chocolate chunks (or chips).

5. Pour the brownie mix into the baking tray, keeping a little aside to swirl on top of the cheesecake mix.

FOR THE CHEESECAKE

6. Add the cream cheese to a bowl and beat to soften (an electric whisk works best). Add the caster sugar and beat again until combined, then gradually beat in the egg and vanilla extract.

7. At this point, I melt some white chocolate and fold it into the cheesecake mix, but this step is optional.

8. Pour the cheesecake mix over the brownie mix before adding dollops of the remaining brownie mix to the tray. Swirl the extra brownie and cheesecake together to create patterns (you may need to get under the mixture to bring the brownie mix to the top).

9. Bake in the oven for 30 to 40 minutes until there is a light wobble in the centre of the brownie. Once baked, leave to cool in the tin before placing in the fridge for 5 to 6 hours or overnight. (Everyone wants to dig straight into their brownies, but trust me, it's worth the wait!)

10. Cut into portions and keep the brownies stored in the fridge so they stay extra fudgy!

Throwbacks

Everybody loves a classic dessert, and all of these recipes have that nostalgia hit that we love. They're popular for a reason, and people go back to them time and time again. We took some of our favourite throwback recipes and added our own Dolly's twist – we like to think of them more as modern classics.

Banana Split

A firm staple on our menu since the beginning. We once took it off the menu and had so many requests for it to be re-added, so we knew we had to include it in the book! Use the classic combo of vanilla, chocolate and strawberry ice cream for a traditional sundae or any flavours of your choice - it really works any way.

PREP TIME: 5 MINUTES | SERVES 1

Ingredients

1 large banana

3 scoops of any flavour ice cream

Squirty cream

Strawberry sauce

Dolly's Milk Chocolate Dessert Sauce

Chopped nuts or sprinkles

3 glacé cherries

Method

1. With the peel still on the banana, slice it vertically down the middle. We keep the skin on for this bit as it can break if it's been peeled.
2. Once you have two halves, carefully peel the skin off each slice and pop them into a long, oval dish.
3. Place 3 scoops in a row in the centre of the banana.
4. Add little squirts of cream at the top and bottom of both sides of each scoop.
5. Drizzle with both the strawberry and chocolate sauce.
6. Add the nuts or sprinkles and top each scoop with a glacé cherry.
7. Serve straight away with a long spoon.

Tip: Make sure to use big bananas - this gives you more space for toppings and will really give this classic dessert the wow factor!

Sticky Toffee Pudding

When we think of a classic dessert, this is one of the first that comes to mind!
A favourite any time of the year, whether it's served with ice cream on a warm
summer's day or comforting custard when it's freezing outside, this spongy
pudding is absolutely delicious and so easy to make!

PREP TIME: 20 MINUTES | COOKING TIME: 40 MINUTES | SERVES 9

Ingredients

100g butter, softened

70g light soft brown sugar

220g self-raising flour

1 tsp bicarbonate of soda

1 tsp baking powder

1 tsp ground ginger

1 tsp ground cinnamon

2 large eggs

3 tbsp black treacle

270ml milk

Dolly's Caramel Gold Sauce, to serve

Method

1. Preheat the oven to 160°c and grease and line a 20x20cm baking tin.

2. In a bowl, cream together the butter and sugar.

3. Sift in the flour, bicarbonate of soda, baking powder and stir to combine.

4. Now it's time to add the ginger and cinnamon - this is going to make your kitchen smell unreal!

5. Mix in the eggs, followed by the black treacle, with a hand whisk.

6. Add the milk a little at a time and stir through to make a smooth batter.

7. Pour the batter in the tray and bake in the oven for 40 minutes.

8. Cut into your desired portion sizes (we think squares look the best).

9. Serve with custard or vanilla ice cream and top with Dolly's Caramel Gold Sauce.

Tip: This can be stored in an airtight container for up to 4 days in the fridge. To reheat, pop it in the microwave for 45 seconds and you've got the perfect pudding any time you like!

Bueno Flapjack

This quick and easy recipe tastes like classic flapjack but taken to the next level! Chewy and delicious, they're the perfect snack - especially for Bueno fans!

PREP TIME: 15 MINUTES, PLUS 6 HOURS CHILLING | COOKING TIME: 30 MINUTES | MAKES 9-12

Ingredients

180g salted butter

190g light soft brown sugar

190g golden syrup

375g porridge oats

400g white chocolate hazelnut spread

100g Nutella

Kinder chocolate, sliced, to decorate (like Bueno and Maxi bars)

Method

1. Preheat the oven to 160°c then line and grease a 20x20cm baking tin.

2. Place the butter, sugar and golden syrup in a pan and melt over a low heat until all the sugar has dissolved.

3. Take off the heat and add the oats, folding until evenly covered.

4. Pour into the baking tin and press down firmly using the back of a spoon or bottom of a glass.

5. Bake for around 30 minutes, then allow to cool for 3 hours to harden.

6. Melt the white chocolate hazelnut spread in the microwave in 20-second bursts then pour it over flapjack. Spread it out evenly and to all the edges using a spatula.

7. Melt the Nutella using the same method, then pour it into a piping bag.

8. Carefully pipe diagonal lines on top of the flapjack, then take a sharp knife or skewer and feather the Nutella, going back and forth in opposite directions.

9. Decorate with Kinder chocolate and put in the fridge for up to 3 hours to set.

10. Slice into portions of your choice, then store in an airtight container in a cool, dark place for up to 1 week.

Tip: Switch out the white chocolate hazelnut spread for any other shop-bought spread of your choice.

Caramel Cornflake Brownie

Just wow on every single level. Soft fudgy brownie topped with the perfect toffee crunch of sticky corn flakes. Everyone loves these so much at Dolly's, and it's always one of the first flavours to sell out. I can see why…

PREP TIME: 15 MINUTES, PLUS 4 HOURS CHILLING | COOKING TIME: 25 MINUTES | MAKES 9-12

Ingredients

180g caster sugar

95g light soft brown sugar

185g salted butter, melted

3 eggs

1 tsp vanilla extract

50g cocoa powder

100g plain flour

200g good quality dark chocolate

100g milk chocolate chips

500g caramel spread (see page 187) or 500g toffees

100ml evaporated milk

120g cornflakes

Method

1. Preheat the oven to 180°c then line and grease a 24x24cm baking tin.

2. In a large bowl, using a mixer or handheld whisk, combine the sugars and butter.

3. Add the eggs and vanilla then mix until combined.

4. Add the cocoa powder carefully, making sure it's mixed evenly throughout the mix.

5. Gradually sift in the flour and mix until fully incorporated.

6. Melt the dark chocolate in 20-second bursts in a microwave and add it to the batter. (Yes, dark chocolate! It's not everyone's favourite, but trust me when I say no brownie is worth eating if it's not made using dark chocolate. It makes the most gooey and rich brownie.)

7. Mix in the milk chocolate chips, then pour the batter into the baking tin and bake for 20 to 25 minutes.

8. If using toffees, unwrap them all and pop into a large microwaveable bowl with the milk, or put the caramel spread in a bowl on its own if using.

9. Heat in the microwave in 30-second intervals, stirring until fully melted. (Careful, these will be super hot!)

10. Fold the cornflakes through until fully coated.

11. Spread the cornflakes evenly over the brownie and press down so it's really compact on top.

12. Put the tray in the fridge to set for at least 4 hours before chopping into portions and enjoying!

Tip: Why not switch the melted toffees for melted chocolate?!

Billionaires Shortbread

This is by far one of my mum's favourites, but it has to have the thickest possible shortbread base! This recipe is based on the classic, but you can switch it up with white chocolate ganache, Biscoff, or Nutella. It's thick and tasty but oh-so simple to make.

PREP TIME: 15 MINUTES, PLUS 2 HOURS CHILLING | COOKING TIME: 30 MINUTES | MAKES 9

Ingredients

450g unsalted butter, room temperature

120g granulated sugar

1 egg yolk

1 tsp vanilla extract

580g plain flour

770g Caramel Spread (see page 187)

480g dark chocolate

160ml double cream

Golden sprinkles, to decorate

Method

1. Preheat the oven to 160°c and grease and line a 20x20cm baking tray.
2. Beat the butter and sugar together until smooth and creamy.
3. Add the egg yolk and vanilla extract and stir until fully combined.
4. Sift in the flour in stages, mixing each time with a spatula until you get a lovely dough.
5. Place the dough into the tray and firmly pat it down using any flat heavy object (like a glass), ensuring it's spread out evenly and to all the edges.
6. Pierce the surface all over with a fork then bake for 20 to 25 minutes until cooked through and golden. Remove from the oven and set aside to cool.
7. Make the caramel then pour it over the cooled shortbread, making sure it covers it evenly. Place in the fridge to cool until it's firm to the touch.
8. Add the chocolate and cream to a pan and place it on a medium heat. Whisk continuously until the chocolate has completely melted and the ingredients are fully combined.
9. Pour over the set caramel and spread with a spatula until smooth and even.
10. Top with golden sprinkles (or even a few cheeky Magic Stars) and pop in the fridge for a couple of hours, or until the chocolate topping is set.
11. Slice and enjoy!

Tip: To get a nice, even cut, dip a really sharp knife into hot water before making each slice.

Birthday Cake Stuffed Cookie

It doesn't have to be someone's birthday for you to make this colourful treat. These cookies are a firm favourite in our bakes cabinet and always sell out so quickly - we knew they had to make a feature in our book!

PREP TIME: 20 MINUTES, PLUS 6 HOURS CHILLING | COOKING TIME: 15 MINUTES | SERVES: 6

Ingredients

6 tbsp White Chocolate Spread, rolled into six even balls (see page 188)

115g butter, softened

160g light brown sugar

40g caster sugar

1 egg

2 tsp vanilla extract

320g plain flour

1 tsp baking powder

1 tsp bicarbonate of soda

200g white chocolate chips

100g bright sprinkles

Method

1. Place the white chocolate spread balls onto a lined baking tray and freeze for at least 30 minutes.
2. Whisk the softened butter, light brown sugar and caster sugar together using an electric whisk until soft and fluffy.
3. Add the egg and vanilla and whisk again until combined.
4. Sift in the flour, baking powder and bicarbonate of soda, then mix with a spatula or cookie rod to form a dough.
5. Add 100g of the white chocolate chips and 75g of the sprinkles, then combine.
6. Separate the dough into six equal portions and roll into balls. Once you have six cookie dough balls, flatten them with your hand and add a frozen ball of chocolate spread into the centre of each cookie. Then, wrap the cookie dough around the spread to form six equal stuffed cookies.
7. Place the cookies on a lined baking tray and freeze for at least 3 hours.
8. Bake in a preheated oven for 9 minutes at 180°c or until the cookies turn golden.
9. Allow to cool for around 2 hours.
10. Melt the remaining chocolate chips and pour small amounts on each cookie to create a drip effect.
11. Sprinkle the remaining sprinkles over the chocolate and pop the cookies in the fridge to set.
12. After about 30 minutes, when the chocolate is set, remove them from the fridge and serve.

Tip: These cookies can be stored in an airtight container in a cool place for up to 5 days, although they're best eaten straight away. Why not warm them through in the microwave a few seconds before serving?

Chocolate & Strawberry Brownie Pots

Fudgy brownie, fresh strawberries, chocolatey custard, and whipped cream. This one's a super quick and easy last-minute dessert, everyone is going to love this modern twist on the classic trifle. Serve in wine glasses for an impressive after-dinner dessert.

PREP TIME: 10 MINUTES | COOKING TIME: 2 MINUTES | SERVES 4

Ingredients

750g brownies, or however much you fancy (see page 74)

500ml ready-made custard

200g dark chocolate, chopped (or chips)

450ml double cream

500g fresh strawberries, sliced

100g milk chocolate, finely grated

Method

1. Start by chopping the brownies into small cubes and distributing half of them between four glasses.

2. In a microwaveable bowl, melt the custard and the chocolate together, stirring every 20 seconds, until smooth and combined. Set aside and allow to cool.

3. In a separate bowl, whisk the double cream to form stiff peaks, but don't over do it - it still needs to be quite soft!

4. Layer half the custard and chocolate mixture into the glasses, then arrange a layer of sliced strawberries neatly around the inside of the glass.

5. Spoon in some of the whipped cream then smooth it out.

6. Add another layer of strawberries to the glasses, then layer all the remaining brownie pieces on top.

7. Divide the remaining chocolate custard between the glasses then finish with the remaining whipped cream (you can use a piping bag for the cream, if you're feeling fancy.)

8. Sprinkle over the grated milk chocolate and add any remaining strawberries. Serve straight away!

Tip: This recipe is so versatile! Try swapping out the brownie for any chocolate cake or muffin and the strawberries with another berry (or even Maltesers for extra indulgence).

Cinnamon Swirl Blondie Pies

These bakes just absolutely scream autumn! We are that cinnamon obsessed
that we use it to make gelato, drinks, cookies, and what we think is the best way
to use it... blondies. The whole house will smell amazing when you make these.
Fudgy blondie pies stuffed with swirled cinnamon sugar are honestly perfection.

PREP TIME: 10 MINUTES, PLUS 8 HOURS CHILLING | COOKING TIME: 20 MINUTES | MAKES 6

Ingredients

FOR THE BLONDIE

190g unsalted butter, softened

125g caster sugar

75g light soft brown sugar

3 eggs, plus 1 egg yolk

1 tsp vanilla extract

340g plain flour

1 tsp salt

2 tsp ground cinnamon

200g white chocolate chips

FOR THE CINNAMON SWIRL

110g light soft brown sugar

75g unsalted butter, melted

3 tsp ground cinnamon

FOR THE ICING

65g icing sugar

2 tsp double cream

1 tsp vanilla extract

Method

1. Preheat the oven to 180°c and grease six small pie tins (we use 300ml aluminium foil tins).

2. In a bowl, cream together the butter, caster sugar and light soft brown sugar.

3. Add eggs and vanilla extract, then mix until light and fluffy. (You may have to mix for a while to get it the perfect consistency.)

4. Sift in the flour, salt and cinnamon and mix again until fully incorporated.

5. In a bowl, melt the white chocolate in 20-second bursts in the microwave and stir through the blondie batter.

6. Evenly distribute the batter between the pie tins and set aside while you make the cinnamon swirl mixture.

7. For the cinnamon swirl, combine the light soft brown sugar, melted butter and cinnamon, then pop it into a piping bag.

8. Pipe deep swirls into each pie then bake in the oven for 20 minutes.

9. Once cooled, pop the blondies in the fridge for at least 4 hours to fully set.

10. Once set, combine the icing sugar, cream, and vanilla in a small bowl.

11. Add to a piping bag, cut a small opening, and pipe the icing all over the cinnamon blondie pies

12. Allow to set in the fridge for 4 hours and enjoy!

Campfire Millionaires

Combining the irresistible flavours of traditional s'mores with the richness of millionaires shortbread, these are a masterpiece. The toasted marshmallow really hits different when paired with the caramel and fudgy brownie. If there's one thing from this book I want you to try, it is this! Plus, it's so easy and looks impressive.

PREP TIME: 20 MINUTES, PLUS 9 HOURS 30 MINUTES CHILLING | COOKING TIME: 20 MINUTES | MAKES 9

Ingredients

FOR THE BROWNIE

140g caster sugar

70g light soft brown sugar

145g salted butter, melted

2 eggs, plus 1 egg yolk

40g cocoa powder

80g plain flour

1 tsp salt

150g dark chocolate

FOR THE TOPPING

770g Caramel Spread (see page 187)

380g dark chocolate

100g milk chocolate

160ml double cream

20 medium-sized marshmallows

90g digestive biscuits, crushed

Method

1. Line and grease a 24x24cm baking tin and preheat the oven to 180°c.

2. Add the caster sugar, soft brown sugar and melted butter to a mixing bowl and cream together until smooth.

3. Add the eggs and extra egg yolk and stir to combine.

4. Gradually sift in the cocoa powder, flour and salt and fold in until fully combined.

5. Melt the dark chocolate in 20-second bursts in the microwave, then mix the melted chocolate into the batter.

6. Transfer to the baking tin and smooth out so it evenly covers the base, then bake for 18 to 20 minutes.

7. Allow to cool then refrigerate for at least 8 hours. (I know it's a long time, but trust me - you want the brownie to set properly!)

8. Once set, gently warm the caramel and pour it over the brownie, making sure it's spread out evenly. Return to the fridge for 30 minutes to set.

9. Melt the dark and milk chocolate together in a bowl, either in 20-second bursts in the microwave or over a pot of simmering water.

10. Add the double cream and stir to combine before pouring it over the top of the set caramel.

11. Roughly distribute the marshmallows and crushed digestive biscuits over the top, then pop back into the fridge for a final hour.

12. Slice and enjoy!

Tip: If you can, try blow-torching your marshmallows! It really gives it that campfire taste!

Caramel Freddo Crispy Muffins

Who doesn't love this little guy? This quick and easy recipe is a must for all the family. The Freddo can easily be replaced by a Flake or any other chocolate bar - just don't let him hear you say that!

PREP TIME: 20 MINUTES, PLUS 3 HOURS CHILLING | COOKING TIME: 5 MINUTES | MAKES 10

Ingredients

210g milk chocolate

90g dark chocolate

80g golden syrup

60g salted butter

140g Rice Krispies

200g Caramel Spread (see page 187)

10 Freddo bars

FOR THE CARAMEL FROSTING

150g salted butter, softened

150g icing sugar

100g caramel sauce, plus extra for drizzling

Method

1. Grease a large, deep muffin tray.

2. Melt the milk and dark chocolate, golden syrup, and butter in a heatproof bowl over a pan of simmering water until silky smooth. You could also use a microwave, heating in 20-second bursts, if it's easier!

3. Add the Rice Krispies to the melted chocolate and stir until fully coated, then evenly distribute around the holes of the muffin tray.

4. Take a rolling pin, or something similar, and make a deep pocket in the middle of each crispy muffin (this should push the mixture to the top and sides), then refrigerate for 1 hour.

5. Fill a piping bag with the Caramel Spread and pipe a dollop into the centre of each crispy muffin case.

6. To make the frosting, cream the butter in a bowl until it becomes light and fluffy (this is the key to making great buttercream).

7. Gradually sift in the icing sugar, little by little, and mix until fully combined. Add the caramel sauce and fold through to make a caramel frosting.

8. Transfer the frosting into a piping bag (using whichever nozzle shape you'd like) and carefully pipe the frosting onto the muffins using a circular motion. We recommend starting from the centre and working your way out to the edge.

9. Drizzle some extra caramel sauce over the muffins, then cut each Freddo bar in half ready to decorate (sorry, Freddo, you just fit better this way!). Top all the muffins with a Freddo so it looks like he's sitting on top of the frosting.

10. Refrigerate for 2 hours and enjoy!

Tip: If you can get your hands on Caramel Freddos, they will take these muffins to the next level!

Liv's Lemon & Pistachio Cake

Hi, I'm Liv! I'm a member of the online team at Dolly's, and lemon drizzle is my go-to for any occasion. You don't have to be an expert baker to make this one look good! My recipe takes the classic to a whole new level, with the addition of roasted pistachios and sweet white chocolate perfectly complementing the tangy lemon.

PREP TIME: 15 MINUTES | COOKING TIME: 1 HOUR | SERVES 10

Ingredients

FOR THE CAKE

3 large eggs (approx 175g)

175g golden caster sugar

175g butter, melted

175g self-raising flour

3 lemons, zested

100g roasted pistachios, shelled and chopped (approx 175g including shells)

FOR THE LEMON DRIZZLE CRUNCH

3 lemons, juiced

175g granulated sugar

TO DECORATE

50g White Chocolate Spread (see page 188)

50g white chocolate chips

Method

1. Preheat the oven to 180°c and grease and line a 2lb loaf tin with greaseproof paper.

2. Add the eggs and sugar to a bowl and beat them until they become light and fluffy. They should become glossy and double in size. (We like to use an electric hand whisk to do this!)

3. Ensure the melted butter has cooled slightly, then pour it into the bowl, mixing continuously, until fully incorporated.

4. Sift in the flour and fold it through, but be careful to not over-mix!

5. Fold in most of the lemon zest and chopped pistachios, using a figure of eight motion so you don't remove the air from the cake batter. Leave a little of both aside to decorate the top of the cake later.

6. Pour the mixture into the lined tin and bake for 45 to 60 minutes or until golden-brown on top. Insert a skewer into the top of the cake, and if it comes out clean, the cake is cooked.

7. While the cake is nearing the end of its baking time, prepare the lemon drizzle crunch. Add the lemon juice to the granulated sugar and mix until incorporated.

8. When ready, remove the cake from the oven and leave to cool slightly. While still warm, use a skewer to poke holes into the top of the cake and drizzle the lemon and sugar mixture over. Leave the cake to cool fully.

9. Once cooled, remove from the tin. You can serve the cake as is, but we like to decorate ours!

10. Melt the white chocolate chips and White Chocolate Spread together in the microwave for 30 seconds. Once melted, drizzle over the top of the loaf cake.

11. Sprinkle with the remaining chopped pistachios and lemon zest to decorate.

Caramel & Jam Cornflake Blondie

Sticky caramel and sweet jam paired with a gooey blondie - this combo is just amazing. This much-loved old school cornflake tart has had a Dolly's makeover! We've changed the pastry to a fudgy blondie, and I'm sure you'll love this version.

PREP TIME: 15 MINUTES, PLUS 1 HOUR CHILLING | COOKING TIME: 25 MINUTES | MAKES 9

Ingredients

190g unsalted butter, melted

125g caster sugar

75g light soft brown sugar

2 eggs, plus 1 egg yolk

1 tsp vanilla extract

340g plain flour

1 tsp salt

200g white chocolate chips

250g strawberry jam

500g Caramel Spread (see page 187), or 500g toffees

140g cornflakes

Method

1. Preheat the oven to 180°c then grease and line a 24x24cm baking tin.

2. In a large bowl, using a mixer or handheld whisk, combine the butter and sugar until smooth.

3. Add the eggs and vanilla and mix until light and fluffy.

4. Gradually sift in the flour and salt, and mix well again, making sure it's fully incorporated.

5. Melt the white chocolate chips in the microwave in 20-second bursts then fold into the mixture.

6. Evenly spread the batter across the bottom of the baking tin, then bake for 20 to 25 minutes until golden-brown.

7. Allow to cool before spreading the jam evenly across the top.

8. If using toffees, unwrap them all and pop into a large microwaveable bowl with the milk, or put the caramel spread in a bowl on its own if using.

9. Heat in the microwave in 30-second intervals, stirring until fully melted. (Careful, these will be super hot!)

10. In a large bowl, combine the cornflakes and melted caramel until the cornflakes are fully coated with the caramel.

11. Spread the cornflakes on top of the jam and press down to make it compact.

12. Place in the fridge for an hour to set, then chop into nine even slices. Serve and enjoy or pop them in an airtight container and store in a cool, dry place for 7 days.

Tip: Pop the jam in the microwave for a few seconds to make it easier to spread! You can also switch up the strawberry jam with any other flavour, like lemon curd or marmalade.

Anika's Red Velvet Cookie Sandwiches

Hi, I'm Anika, and I'm the manager at Dolly's. I've been here for 6 years and seen the business go from strength to strength! Even though I'm not a baker, I've definitely learned a lot over the years. I've come up with this recipe as I love anything red velvet and white chocolate. I hope you love these cookies as much as I do!

PREP TIME: 20 MINUTES PLUS 2 HOURS COOLING | COOKING TIME: 15 MINUTES | MAKES 6

Ingredients

FOR THE COOKIES

270g light soft brown sugar

130g unsalted butter, softened

2 tsp vanilla extract

2 eggs

1 tsp red food colouring

360g plain flour

2 tbsp cocoa powder

2 tsp baking powder

130g white chocolate chips

FOR THE BUTTERCREAM FILLING

150g unsalted butter, softened

300g icing sugar

80g White Chocolate Spread (see page 188)

Method

1. Preheat the oven to 180°c and line two baking trays with greaseproof paper.

2. In a large bowl, whisk the sugar, softened butter and vanilla until combined.

3. Add the eggs and red food colouring and mix until fully incorporated.

4. Sift in the plain flour, cocoa powder and baking powder, then fold it through. It should start to form a dough - top tip, get your hands in and knead it all together!

5. Add the chocolate chips and mix them all in, then weigh the dough out into 85g balls.

6. Divide the dough balls between the baking trays, flattening them down slightly. You should have about 12 cookies, which will make six cookie sandwiches.

7. Bake in the oven for 10 to 12 minutes. When ready, remove and set aside to cool for a couple of hours.

8. To make the buttercream filling, whisk the softened butter and slowly begin to add the icing sugar, bit by bit. Once combined, add the White Chocolate Spread and whisk it into the butter cream.

9. Add the butter cream to a piping bag and pipe it onto the bottom of one cookie.

10. Sandwich another cookie on top, then repeat the process until all the cookies are sandwiched together! Serve and enjoy!

The Ultimate Christmas Hot Chocolate

The creamiest, most indulgent hot chocolate recipe you will ever try. This takes you right back to being in your pjs, tucked up on the sofa watching a Christmas film. If you're looking for a warming winter treat... you're on the perfect page.

PREP TIME: 5 MINUTES | COOKING TIME: 10 MINUTES | MAKES 1

Ingredients

150ml whole milk

50ml double cream

½ tsp light soft brown sugar

½ orange, zested

1 clove

¼ tsp ground ginger

50g dark chocolate, chopped

2 Lindt chocolate truffles

FOR THE TOPPING

Squirty cream, to serve

Cocoa powder, to dust

1 Lindt chocolate truffle

1 mini gingerbread man

Method

1. Add the milk, cream, sugar, orange zest, clove and ground ginger to a saucepan.
2. Stir gently over a medium heat until it begins to simmer.
3. Allow to simmer for a few minutes so the flavours infuse, then strain over a jug to remove the leftover zest and clove.
4. Pour the spiced milk back into the saucepan and add the dark chocolate.
5. Stir until melted, then add the Lindt chocolate truffles (our faves).
6. Once you have a smooth, silky consistency, pour the hot chocolate into your favourite mug.
7. Top with squirty cream, a dusting of cocoa powder, a Lindt chocolate truffle, and a gingerbread man. Serve and enjoy!

Tip: Sometimes, when you put cream on a hot drink, it can go everywhere and it looks super messy. However, if you hold the can of squirty cream upside down and squirt small sections around the edge of the mug, followed by a bit in the centre, it creates the perfect foundation to add more on top! You're welcome.

Basic Biscuits

Who doesn't love a biscuit? Some are so iconic that we think they'll be around forever. We all have a favourite, and whether you're obsessed with Oreos, Biscoff or Bourbons, there's a recipe in here for you. In this chapter, you will find many recipes that convert basic biscuits into stunning bakes and desserts and - even better - most of them can be swapped and adapted to use whichever biscuit you fancy!

Cookies & Cream Millionaires

Although we say Bueno is the star of the show at Dolly's due to its popularity, Oreos are definitely a strong contender. This twist on the classic millionaires shortbread is a popular one. The rich crunch of the base paired with the gooey caramel is to die for! This is an easy no-bake recipe that everyone can enjoy.

PREP TIME: 15 MINUTES, PLUS 2 HOURS CHILLING | MAKES 9

Ingredients

450g Oreos or cookies and cream biscuits, plus 9 to decorate

120g salted butter, melted

Caramel Spread (see page 187)

250g white chocolate

Method

1. Crush the Oreos in a bowl until they resemble breadcrumbs. (You can use a food processor or pop the Oreos in a sandwich bag and bash them with a rolling pin, if you prefer.)
2. Add the melted butter and combine.
3. Grease and line a 20x20cm baking tin with greaseproof paper.
4. Press the Oreo crumb into the base to create the bottom layer of the millionaires.
5. Next, gently warm the Caramel Spread in the microwave to make it super spreadable, then add it to the Oreo base. Spread it evenly, making sure you cover the whole surface, then refrigerate for 1 hour.
6. Once set, melt the white chocolate and pour it over the tray, again spreading it around evenly.
7. While the chocolate is still liquid, top the millionaires with the whole Oreo biscuits to decorate, then pop in the fridge for another hour to set. (We like to do one Oreo per slice.)
8. Once set, remove from the tin, slice and enjoy!

Tip: You can easily make a Biscoff version of this, too! Use crushed Biscoff biscuits with the butter for the base, then either keep the white chocolate or switch to Biscoff spread – both work extremely well – and finish with small Biscoff biscuits or crumbs.

Nutella Stuffed Cookies

We honestly can't believe how much these have blown up over the last couple of years! We sell out almost every Saturday! These New York-style cookies are crunchy on the outside with a sweet, gooey centre - we could eat these all day long. When you make them, we're sure you'll understand why.

PREP TIME: 15 MINUTES, PLUS 3 HOURS 30 MINUTES FREEZING | COOKING TIME: 10 MINUTES | MAKES 6

Ingredients

9 tbsp Nutella

115g butter, softened

160g light soft brown sugar

40g caster sugar

1 egg

2 tsp vanilla extract

320g plain flour

1 tsp baking powder

1 tsp bicarbonate of soda

150g milk chocolate chips

Method

1. Place 9 separate tablespoons of Nutella onto a lined baking tray, making sure they are spaced out evenly, and freeze for at least 30 minutes.
2. Whisk the butter, light soft brown sugar and caster sugar using an electric whisk until soft and fluffy.
3. Add the egg and the vanilla and whisk again until combined.
4. Sift in the flour, baking powder and bicarbonate of soda into the bowl, then mix with a spatula or cookie rod to form a dough.
5. Scatter in the chocolate chips and knead them through the dough.
6. Dust the countertop with some flour and place the dough on top (this will keep the dough from sticking). Cut the dough into six equal portions and roll each one into a ball.
7. Lightly flatten each ball using the palm of your hand then pop a frozen Nutella ball into the centre of each.
8. Wrap the dough around the Nutella to make six Nutella-stuffed cookie dough balls.
9. Place the cookies on a lined baking tray and freeze for at least 3 hours before baking at 180°c for 9 minutes, or until the cookies are golden-brown.
10. Allow to cool, then serve and enjoy!

Tip: Instead of Nutella, try placing a whole Cadbury's Creme or Caramel Egg inside for an impressive Easter treat.

Bueno Bliss Cookie Dough

The best-selling cookie dough in store by an absolute country mile. We must make hundreds of these on a weekend, and it's definitely a customer favourite! Kinder Buenos are one of our go-to chocolate bars, and when combined with hot cookie dough, they really make the most heavenly combo.

PREP TIME: 10 MINUTES | COOKING TIME: 12 MINUTES | SERVES 2

Ingredients

200g salted butter, softened

200g light soft brown sugar

1 egg

2 tsp vanilla extract

225g plain flour

2 tsp baking powder

Splash of milk, if required

100g milk chocolate, chopped into small chunks

1 Kinder Bueno

2 Kinder Maxi

Dolly's Bueno Dessert Sauce, to serve

Method

1. Preheat the oven to 180°c.

2. In a bowl, cream together the softened butter and sugar.

3. Add the egg and vanilla extract, then stir to combine.

4. Sift in the flour and baking powder, then mix until all the ingredients come together and start to resemble a dough. Add a splash of milk, if needed, to ensure a smooth dough that's not too wet, and not too dry.

5. Fold the chocolate chunks through the dough then divide it into four equal portions - two layers for each dish.

6. Line two small oven dishes (we like to use skillets) and press a portion of dough into the base of each. Flatten it out to the edges to ensure even coverage.

7. Break up the Kinder Bueno bar and distribute it on top of the first layer of dough.

8. Use the remaining portions of cookie dough to cover the Bueno pieces. (You don't want any Kinder Bueno showing as the wafer can burn while baking).

9. Decorate the top with the Kinder Maxi chocolate bars and bake for 10 to 12 minutes until golden.

10. Leave to stand for a couple of minutes, then drizzle with Dolly's Bueno Dessert Sauce and serve with a large scoop of vanilla ice cream.

Custard Cream Rocky Road

This recipe looks SO impressive. The custard-flavoured chocolate and the iconic custard cream are perfectly matched, and when they're sandwiched together with marshmallows, want more could you ever want or need?

PREP TIME: 20 MINUTES, PLUS 2 HOURS CHILLING | COOKING TIME: 5 MINUTES | MAKES 9

Ingredients

350g custard cream biscuits

120g mini marshmallows

600g white chocolate

50g custard powder

100g unsalted butter

Method

1. Line a 20x20cm baking tin. Set six custard creams aside for decoration, then chop the remaining biscuits into bite-sized pieces and transfer to a large mixing bowl with the marshmallows.

2. Carefully melt the white chocolate in the microwave in 20-second bursts, then stir in the custard powder.

3. Melt the butter and add it to the custard-flavoured chocolate, then add this to the crushed biscuits and marshmallows. Stir until fully combined.

4. Press the mixture into the baking tin, ensuring it's evenly spread out into all the corners.

5. Spilt the six remaining custard cream biscuits in half to make 12 thin biscuits, then arrange them on top to decorate.

6. Place in the fridge to cool for at least a couple of hours, then use a sharp knife to cut into portions.

Tip: Run a sharp knife under a hot tap before slicing to ensure lovely, clean cuts. Store in an airtight container in a cool place for up to 10 days.

Jammie Dodger Blondies

These are one of our most popular blondies in store and one of the first to sell out! The combination of soft, chewy blondie with a ripple of jam and Jammie Dodger biscuit is just perfect.

PREP TIME: 10 MINUTES, PLUS 8 HOURS COOLING | COOKING TIME: 25 MINUTES | MAKES 9

Ingredients

190g unsalted butter, softened

125g caster sugar

200g light soft brown sugar

3 eggs

1 tsp vanilla extract

310g plain flour

200g white chocolate chips

16 Jammie Dodgers

270g strawberry jam

Method

1. Preheat the oven to 180ºc and grease and line a 20x20cm baking tray.

2. In a bowl, mix the softened butter, caster sugar and light brown sugar together until soft and creamy.

3. Add the eggs and vanilla extract then mix again until light and fluffy.

4. Sift in the flour then gently fold until combined.

5. Melt the white chocolate in the microwave in 20-second bursts (be careful not to burn it!), then add it to the bowl and mix well until combined.

6. Add half the blondie batter into the baking tray and smooth it out evenly to the edges.

7. Place half the Jammie Dodgers on top of the batter, then add little blobs of jam to the gaps in-between the biscuits.

8. Add the remaining batter and spread it out evenly.

9. Add the remaining strawberry jam to a piping bag (or sandwich bag if you don't have one). Cut a small hole into the tip of the bag and pipe the jam onto the blondie batter in diagonal lines.

10. Drag a sharp knife through the lines in the opposite direction to create a feathered pattern, the top with the remaining Jammie Dodgers.

11. Pop in the oven and bake for 25 minutes.

12. Let the blondies cool, then pop them in the fridge overnight or for at least 8 hours to properly set. Slice into nine portions and enjoy!

Biscoff Hot Chocolate

Biscoff lovers, this one's for you! Honestly, this is the easiest recipe ever - literally anyone can make it, and it goes down such a treat on an autumn or winter's day.

PREP TIME: 5 MINUTES | COOKING TIME: 5 MINUTES | SERVES 2

Ingredients

500ml milk (whichever type you prefer)

6 tbsp Biscoff spread

100g white chocolate

Whipped cream, to serve

4 Biscoff biscuits (2 whole; 2 crushed)

Method

1. Add the milk, Biscoff spread and white chocolate to a saucepan over a low heat, stirring continuously until the spread and chocolate have melted (but making sure to not let it boil).

2. Once smooth, fully incorporated, and warmed through, remove from the heat and pour into two mugs.

3. Top with whipped cream and Biscoff biscuit crumbs and serve with a whole biscuit.

Tip: Place a couple of teaspoons of Biscoff spread into the microwave for 10 seconds then drizzle over the top for an even more indulgent drink! Switching to Nutella will make an equally impressive and comforting drink.

Bourbon No-bake Cheesecake

How can we possibly make one of the nation's most loved biscuits better? Make it into a cheesecake! This one's quick, easy and looks so impressive!

PREP TIME: 15 MINUTES, PLUS 4 HOURS CHILLING TIME | SERVES 8

Ingredients

450g Bourbon biscuits

90g butter, melted

250ml double cream

350ml cream cheese

1 tsp vanilla extract

120g icing sugar

110g dark chocolate

Method

1. Crush 180g of the Bourbon biscuits using a food processor (or you can always use a trusty rolling pin and sandwich bag!).
2. Add the biscuit crumbs and melted butter to a bowl and combine.
3. Line an 8-inch cake tin with greaseproof paper then line the edges with the remaining whole Bourbon biscuits, with each biscuit standing vertically.
4. Add the biscuit and butter base to the tin and press it down firmly and evenly.
5. In a bowl, whisk the double cream until it forms stiff peaks.
6. In another bowl, add the cream cheese, vanilla extract, and icing sugar and mix until combined.
7. Melt the dark chocolate in the microwave in 20-second bursts then stir it through the cream cheese mixture.
8. Fold in the whipped cream, then transfer the cheesecake filling to the cake tin and smooth it out evenly.
9. Chill the cheesecake in the fridge for at least 4 hours, then slice and enjoy!

Giant Celebration Cookie

Show someone you care by making them this cookie! We sold loads of these in lockdown, and they did the best job of putting a massive smile on your loved ones' faces. I mean, who doesn't love a giant cookie? Literally any message can be written on this, so it's perfect for any occasion!

PREP TIME: 15 MINUTES, PLUS 30 MINUTES COOLING AND DECORATING TIME | COOKING TIME: 15 MINUTES | SERVES 8

Ingredients

FOR THE COOKIE

90g unsalted butter, softened

50g caster sugar

110g light soft brown sugar

1 egg

½ tsp vanilla extract

140g plain flour

½ tsp salt

¼ tsp bicarbonate of soda

00g white or milk chocolate chunks or chips

FOR THE BUTTERCREAM

100g unsalted butter, softened

1 tsp vanilla extract

200g icing sugar

Gel-based food colourings (of your choice)

Method

1. Preheat the oven to 180°c then line and grease a 10-inch cake tin (we use a springform tin as it makes it easier to get the cookie out at the end!).
2. To make the cookie, combine the softened butter and both sugars in a large mixing bowl.
3. Add the egg and vanilla extract, then mix again.
4. Sift in the plain flour, salt, and bicarbonate of soda and mix to form a dough.
5. Add the chocolate chips or chunks and fold them into the dough.
6. Press and flatten the dough into the cake tin, spreading it evenly across the base.
7. Bake in the oven for 15 minutes until golden-brown. Knock the air out of the cookie by tapping the cake tin on the work surface a couple of times, then allow it to cool.
8. Carefully remove the cookie from the tin and place it on a cooling rack. Once cooled (about 30 minutes), it's time to start decorating.
9. To make the buttercream, add the butter and vanilla to a bowl and whisk until light and fluffy (this should be light in colour too!).
10. Carefully sift in the icing sugar, little by little, and mix until fully combined. The buttercream should be light and airy when done.
11. Split the buttercream into batches and add a drop of gel-based colouring to each batch. Mix well, add more drops if necessary, and distribute into piping bags.
12. Decorate your cookie however you wish! We recommend writing your message first before you do the edges to avoid smudging. Get creative with different piping nozzles and toppings!

Tip: Use pre-made chocolate letters to spell out your message for a neater look – just place a little buttercream under each letter to make sure it sticks!

HAPPY BIRTHDAY
Congratulations

Nutella Stuffed Crookies

We're sure you've all seen the viral cookie dough croissant. This quick and easy recipe uses shop-bought croissants… I mean, who has the time to make croissants from scratch? If you have got time, that's amazing (we're jealous), but if not this works perfectly, too!

PREP TIME: 10 MINUTES | COOKING TIME: 15 MINUTES | SERVES 6

Ingredients

150g salted butter, softened

85g caster sugar

30g light soft brown sugar

1 egg

270g plain flour

100g milk chocolate chips

100g dark chocolate chips

6 good quality croissants

6 tbsp Nutella

Method

1. Preheat the oven to 180ºc and line a large baking tray.
2. In a bowl, mix the softened butter, caster sugar and soft brown sugar until creamy.
3. Add the egg and mix again until fully combined.
4. Carefully sift in the flour and fold it through until it forms a dough.
5. Add the chocolate chips and mix together - don't be scared to get your hands in to mix this!
6. Slice the croissants in half and spread each one with 1 tablespoon of Nutella.
7. Place a flattened layer of cookie dough inside each croissant and then another piece of cookie dough on top of the croissant. (Make sure you're even with your portions!)
8. Once all the croissants are prepped and ready, place them on the baking tray and bake for 15 minutes.
9. Allow to cool slightly before serving warm! (We are so obsessed with these - enjoy!)

Tip: Switch up the Nutella and milk and dark chocolate chips for Biscoff spread and white chocolate chips.

Cookies & Cream Stuffed Cookies

We just love the colour and texture of these cookies. There's so much going on in each mouthful! These are new to our menu and we are absolutely sure they're here to stay!

PREP TIME: 10 MINUTES, PLUS 3 HOURS 30 MINUTES FREEZING | COOKING TIME: 15 MINUTES | MAKES 6

Ingredients

6 tbsp cookies and cream spread

115g butter, softened

160g light soft brown sugar

40g caster sugar

1 egg

1 tsp vanilla extract

320g plain flour

1 tsp baking powder

1 tsp bicarbonate of soda

170g white chocolate chips

150g Oreos, crushed

50g milk chocolate spread

6 Oreos, whole

Method

1. Roll the tablespoons of cookies and cream spread into balls and place on a lined baking tray. Freeze for at least 30 minutes.

2. Cream the softened butter, light brown sugar and caster sugar together using an electric whisk until light and fluffy.

3. Add the egg and vanilla extract then whisk again until combined.

4. Sift in the flour, baking powder and bicarbonate of soda then mix with a spatula to form a dough.

5. Fold in the white chocolate chips, then cut the dough into six equal portions. Roll into six balls, then flatten them out.

6. Place a ball of frozen spread into the centre of each, then wrap the dough around the spread to form a ball. Make sure all the spread is covered, then roll each ball in the Oreo crumbs.

7. Place the cookies back on the lined baking tray and freeze for 3 hours.

8. Bake in a preheated oven for 12 to 14 minutes at 180°c, then allow to cool.

9. Once cooled, melt the milk chocolate spread for about 40 seconds, then pour it over each cookie.

10. Finish each cookie with a whole Oreo, then place them in the fridge for about 30 minutes until the spread has hardened. Serve and enjoy!

Tip: Switch out the cookies and cream spread and Oreos for Biscoff spread and biscuits for a totally different taste!

Cookie Monster Milkshake

A total staple in our store on the Dolly's Shakes menu. This vibrant milkshake is a show-stopper for sure and goes down a treat with the kids! A thick cookies and cream milkshake with an iconic blue colour for the real cookie monsters out there.

PREP TIME: 10 MINUTES | SERVES 2

Ingredients

200ml whole milk

3 cookies and cream biscuits (we like to use Oreos), plus more to decorate

3 Biscoff biscuits, plus more to decorate

6 scoops vanilla ice cream (shop-bought or see page 176 for our recipe)

Blue food colouring, as needed

Whipped cream, to serve

Method

1. In a blender, add the milk, biscuits, six (healthy!) scoops of vanilla ice cream, and blue food colouring. Make sure to add the milk first, as the blender can struggle and get stuck if you put the ice cream in first. There is no set measurement for the food colouring as it all depends on the brand you use and how vibrant you would like it to be. Personally, I think if you're making this then you should go all out. The brighter, the better!

2. Blend until combined and a thick consistency, then pour into two tall glasses. Try adding a bit of Dolly's sauce round the edge of the glass like the ones we serve in-store.

3. Top with freshly whipped cream and finish with a few smashed Biscoff and cookies and cream biscuits. Serve and enjoy!

Caramel Cookie Brownie

This is our iconic brownie recipe and we're excited to share it with you. We did a lot of trial and error, hard graft, and tweaking to come up with what we think is the best brownie recipe ever. We're certain you'll agree!

PREP TIME: 15 MINUTES, PLUS 8 HOURS CHILLING | COOKING TIME: 25 MINUTES | MAKES 9

Ingredients

185g caster sugar

95g soft brown sugar

185g salted butter, melted

3 eggs

1 tsp vanilla extract

50g cocoa powder

100g plain flour

200g good quality dark chocolate

300g Caramel Spread, room temperature (see page 187)

300g Edible Cookie Dough, or shop-bought cookies (see page 188)

Method

1. Preheat the oven 180°c and line a 20x20cm baking tin. In a large bowl, using a mixer or handheld whisk, combine both sugars and the butter.

2. Add the eggs and vanilla and mix until fully combined.

3. Sift in the cocoa powder, making sure it's mixed evenly throughout the batter. Gradually sift in the flour and mix well until you can see absolutely no white.

4. Melt the chocolate in 20-second bursts in a microwave and add it to the batter. Stir to combine, then place half of the batter into the lined baking tin.

5. Evenly distribute half of the caramel and cookie dough, or cookies, across the whole tin.

6. Spread the remaining batter on top, ensuring everything has a thick covering.

7. Put the remaining caramel into a strong piping bag and pipe it onto the batter in thick strips. Then, use a skewer or the pointy end of a sharp knife to feather it in opposite directions from the strips.

8. Place the rest of the cookie dough, or cookies, in small bite-sized portions across the top. If using pieces of cookie dough, these will spread out during baking to form small cookie puddles.

9. Bake at 180°c for 20 minutes. Don't worry if the brownie still looks jiggly - this is normal.

10. Allow to cool slightly, then refrigerate for at least 8 hours, and preferably overnight. This is really important as the chocolate needs to reset. The finished result should be a firm, gooey fudge-like texture.

11. Remove from the baking tray and chop into squares. These can be stored in the fridge and will still be amazing for up to 10 days.

Tip: The cookie dough can easily be switched out for chocolate chip cookies. Don't be afraid to experiment with different biscuits either.

Maple & Pecan Crumble Cookies

I first tried this flavour combination when I went to Florida. I got a maple and pecan cinnamon bun from Cinnabon and oh, my God... I was so obsessed! I thought we had to do them at Dolly's! This is the perfect combination in our opinion: a soft crumbly pecan cookie topped with a super sweet maple frosting.

PREP TIME: 15 MINUTES | COOKING TIME: 15 MINUTES | MAKES 10

Ingredients

FOR THE COOKIES

250g unsalted butter, softened

135g granulated sugar

1 egg

1 tsp vanilla extract

1 tsp almond essence

385g plain flour

1 tsp baking powder

1 tsp salt

120g pecans

FOR THE FROSTING

100g unsalted butter, softened

200g icing sugar

70g maple syrup

TO DECORATE

1 small handful of pecans, chopped

Ground cinnamon or caramel sauce, to garnish

Method

1. Preheat the oven to 160°c and line two baking trays.
2. In a mixing bowl, cream the butter and sugar together.
3. Add the egg, vanilla extract and almond essence, and combine.
4. Sift in the flour, baking powder, and salt. Mix until combined.
5. Roughly chop the pecans and fold into the cookie dough (we like to leave some big chunks in this to give the cookies a nice crunch).
6. Weigh the dough into ten 100g portions, roll into balls, and place on the baking trays, making sure to keep them spaced apart, as they will spread while they bake.
7. Bake for 12 to 15 minutes until lightly golden, then remove from the oven and cool.
8. To make the frosting, beat the softened butter in a bowl until it becomes light in colour (this is important because it makes your frosting airy and fluffy!).
9. Slowly sift in the icing sugar, a little at a time, and keep mixing until fully combined.
10. Add the maple syrup and mix again.
11. Transfer the frosting to a piping bag and carefully pipe icing onto each cookie. Use a circular motion, starting from the outside and working your way to the centre.
12. Finish with a sprinkling of chopped pecans and some ground cinnamon or a drizzle of caramel sauce for extra sweetness, before serving.

Pistachio & White Chocolate Millionaires

This thick shortbread base is topped with a layer of golden caramel, silky smooth white chocolate, and a toasty pistachio cream in this modern twist on the classic millionaires shortbread. This one's sure to impress – especially if you're pistachio obsessed!

PREP TIME: 20 MINUTES, PLUS 1 HOUR 15 MINUTES CHILLING | COOKING TIME: 30 MINUTES | MAKES 9

Ingredients

450g unsalted butter

120g granulated sugar

1 egg yolk

1 tsp vanilla extract

60g plain flour

Pinch of salt, to taste

770g Caramel Spread (see page 187)

500g pistachio spread

120g white chocolate, roughly chopped

Method

1. Preheat the oven to 160°c then grease and line a 24x24cm baking tin.
2. In a mixing bowl, cream together the butter and sugar until fully combined.
3. Add the egg yolk and vanilla and mix again until smooth.
4. Carefully sift in the flour and salt and fold it into the wet mixture to form a dough (you might want to get your hands dirty for this part).
5. Transfer the dough to the baking tin and press it down firmly to create an even layer.
6. Lightly prick the dough all over the top with a fork and bake for 25 minutes until golden.
7. Remove from the oven and allow to cool.
8. In a separate bowl, warm the Caramel Spread in the microwave (in 20-second bursts) until slightly melted and thin enough to pour.
9. Pour the caramel all over the shortbread and spread it out evenly, then chill in the fridge for at least 30 minutes.
10. When the caramel has nearly set, melt the pistachio spread and white chocolate in separate bowls. Transfer the white chocolate to a piping bag ready to decorate.
11. Pour the pistachio spread over the set caramel and smooth it out evenly, then pipe the melted white chocolate in thick stripes across the tin. Use a skewer or the pointy end of a sharp knife to feather the chocolate in opposite directions.
12. Add any remaining chocolate to the top, if desired, and allow to set in the fridge for another 30 to 40 minutes.
13. Slice into nine portions and enjoy!

Ice Cream

Did you really think that we'd make a cookbook without including some ice cream? It's our most sold thing at Dolly's and has defined our company from the very beginning. If you know us really well, you will know that we technically sell gelato, made using the finest Italian ingredients. Unfortunately, not everyone has access to these or to a big fancy machine, but we still wanted to include some of our favourite recipes. This chapter's full of homemade ice cream versions of Dolly's famous gelato.

Top tips for this chapter:
Run your ice cream scoop under hot water to help achieve the perfect scoop.
Our ice cream recipes are best consumed within 1 to 2 weeks, but they will last longer in the freezer (if you can resist them!).

Hattie's Matilda Cake Semifreddo

This is Hattie's signature twist on the famous chocolate cake from Matilda. Rich chocolate sponge with ice cream… made into a cake! Now you can make it at home, too. Amazing, right?!

PREP TIME: 30 MINUTES, PLUS 4 HOURS FREEZING | COOKING TIME: 40 MINUTES | SERVES 12

Ingredients

FOR THE CHOCOLATE CAKE

250g plain flour

55g cocoa powder

1 tsp baking powder

1 tsp bicarbonate of soda

1 tsp salt

200g caster sugar

110g light soft brown sugar

2 eggs

120ml vegetable or sunflower oil

1 tsp vanilla extract

4 tsp instant coffee, dissolved in 220ml water

FOR THE SEMIFREDDO

420g double cream

165g egg whites

90g caster sugar

1 tsp salt

3 tbsp cocoa powder

150g-200g brownie, broken into pieces (optional)

TO DECORATE

Brownie, broken into pieces

Fresh strawberries, sliced (optional)

Method

FOR THE CHOCOLATE CAKE

1. Preheat the oven to 180ºc and grease and line an 8-inch cake tin.

2. Sift the flour, cocoa powder, baking powder, bicarbonate of soda, and salt into a large mixing bowl, then stir in the caster and soft brown sugar. Add the eggs, oil and vanilla extract, then whisk until combined (it may be quite thick, but this is normal). Slowly add the instant coffee, stirring continuously, until the mixture is smooth.

3. Transfer to the cake tin and bake for 30 to 40 minutes, or until a toothpick comes out clean.. Once baked, allow to cool, then remove from the tin and wrap in cling film. Transfer to the freezer to chill.

4. Once frozen and ready to assemble, slice widthways into three or four layers (this will determine how many layers the cake will have).

FOR THE SEMIFREDDO

1. Whisk the double cream in a mixing bowl until very soft peaks form. There should only be slight resistance when you move it and it should hold the trails from the whisk.

2. Whisk the egg whites, sugar and salt together in a separate bowl to make a meringue. It won't be super stiff, but will hold its peaks.

3. Whisk a tablespoon of the meringue mixture into the semi-whipped cream. Once combined, swap to a spatula and fold in the rest of the meringue mixture, bit by bit, until you get a light and airy mixture.

4. Fold the cocoa powder in 1 tablespoon at a time until fully combined, then fold in the brownie pieces, if including. Be careful not to over-mix or you'll knock too much of the air out!

TO ASSEMBLE

1. Grab a cake board or plate and pop down a layer of cake followed by a layer of chocolate semifreddo. Spread it out evenly and repeat, alternating layers, until you have used up all the cake. Finish with a layer of semifreddo around the whole cake, smoothing it out evenly.

2. Freeze for 3 to 4 hours until fully set. Once frozen, decorate with brownies or strawberries. Leave to soften for 15 minutes and slice.

Biscoff Ice Cream

Who doesn't love Biscoff? This is a firm favourite across all our desserts, and if this is still not enough Biscoff for you, try melting a little bit more to drizzle over the top!

PREP TIME: 15 MINUTES, PLUS 6 HOURS FREEZING | COOKING TIME: 5 MINUTES | MAKES APPROX. 1KG

Ingredients

10-12 Biscoff biscuits

480ml whipping cream

300g Biscoff spread

1 x 397g tin of condensed milk (best chilled)

Method

1. Line a freezer-safe container or loaf tin and add a layer of five or six Biscoff biscuits to the base, depending on the tin's length.

2. Add the cream to a bowl and whisk on full power using an electric whisk until stiff peaks form.

3. Add Biscoff spread into a separate bowl and microwave on medium heat for 20 seconds until melted but not warm (you just want it to be thinner so it can be stirred easily!).

4. Add the condensed milk and 300g of the melted Biscoff spread to the cream and whisk on low power until fully incorporated.

5. Scoop the mixture onto the biscuit base and smooth out to the edges. Top with another layer of five to six biscuits, placed side by side.

6. Cover with cling film and chill in the freezer for a minimum of six hours to fully set.

7. To serve, leave out for 5 to 10 minutes before slicing into portions (you can use the biscuits as markers). Serve and enjoy!

Unicorn Ice Cream

This is so pretty and sure to be a hit with all the princes and princesses out there. We use gel colour as it produces a much brighter colour and puts less unnecessary liquid into the mixture.

PREP TIME: 15 MINUTES, PLUS 6 HOURS FREEZING | MAKES APPROX. 1KG

Ingredients

480ml whipping cream

1 x 397g tin of condensed milk (best chilled)

4 shades of neon food colouring, to decorate (the brighter, the better)

Unicorn sprinkles, to decorate

Method

1. Add the cream to a bowl and whisk on full power using an electric whisk until stiff peaks form.

2. Add the condensed milk to the bowl and whisk on low power until incorporated.

3. Divide the mixture into four bowls, then add a couple of drops of food colouring to each bowl and mix well until there is no white. You may need to keep adding more until you reach the desired colour, but the brighter the better for this one!

4. Scoop even amounts of each colour into a freezer-safe container and swirl using a cocktail stick or sharp knife to marble the colours.

5. Wrap with cling film to ensure no moisture can enter, then chill in the freezer for a minimum of 6 hours.

6. To serve, leave out for 5 to 10 minutes, scoop out, and top with a multi-coloured unicorn sprinkles.

Dolly's
DESSERTS

Salted Caramel Ice Cream

This iconic flavour works so well as a no-churn recipe thanks to the Carnation Caramel. We use double cream in this one as the caramel is naturally a softer texture, so the higher fat content in the cream adds the extra structure this ice cream needs.

PREP TIME: 15 MINUTES, PLUS 6 HOURS FREEZING | MAKES APPROX. 1KG

Ingredients

480ml double cream

1 x 397g tin of Carnation Caramel (best chilled)

200g Caramel Spread (there are no rules if you want to add a bit more!)

Flaky sea salt, to taste

Method

1. Add the double cream to a bowl and whisk on full power using an electric whisk until stiff peaks form.

2. Add the Carnation Caramel to the bowl and whisk on low power until fully incorporated.

3. Scoop half the mixture into a freezer-safe container, then ripple the Caramel Spread through the centre and sprinkle with a pinch of sea salt. Finish with the remaining mixture and smooth out to the edges.

4. Wrap with cling film to ensure no moisture can enter, then put in the freezer for a minimum of 6 hours.

5. To serve, leave out for 5 to 10 minutes before scooping out into a bowl and topping with extra flaky sea salt.

Cookie Dough Ice Cream

Cookie dough and ice cream are a match made in heaven! If you've not made the cookie dough beforehand, you can use cookie pieces - just coat them in melted butter to stop them going soggy in your ice cream (because nobody wants a soggy cookie!).

PREP TIME: 15 MINUTES, PLUS 6 HOURS FREEZING | MAKES APPROX. 1KG

Ingredients

480ml whipping cream

1 fresh vanilla pod, seeds removed, or 1 tsp vanilla extract

1 x 397g tin of condensed milk (best chilled)

Edible Cookie Dough (however much you like, see page 188)

Method

1. Add the cream to a bowl and whisk on full power using an electric whisk until stiff peaks form.
2. Add the vanilla extract or, if using, split the vanilla pod down the centre and scrape out the vanilla seeds.
3. Add the condensed milk and whisk on low power until incorporated.
4. Break the cookie dough into bite-sized pieces and fold through the mixture.
5. Scoop the mixture into a freezer-safe container and smooth out to the edges.
6. Wrap with cling film to ensure no moisture can enter, then chill in the freezer for a minimum of 6 hours.
7. To serve, leave out for 5 to 10 minutes before scooping into bowls and enjoying with your favourite toppings (we love our Dolly's Luxury Dessert Sauces!).

Dolly's
DESSERTS

Bueno & Nutty Ella Ice Cream

This one's our best-selling ice cream, by an absolute country mile, and now you can recreate this much-loved flavour at home!

PREP TIME: 15 MINUTES, PLUS 6 HOURS FREEZING | MAKES APPROX. 1KG

Ingredients

480ml whipping cream

1 x 397g tin of condensed milk

100g Dolly's Bueno Dessert Sauce

100g Dolly's Nutty Ella Dessert Sauce

4 Kinder Maxi bars, chopped into chunks, to decorate

Method

1. Add whipped cream into a bowl and whisk on full power until stiff peaks form.

2. Add the condensed milk to the bowl and whisk on low until it's all incorporated.

3. Place half the mixture in a large tupperware, then add half of each sauce in alternating stripes and feather in the opposite direction using a skewer. Throw in half of the chopped Kinder chocolate bars, then add the rest of the ice cream mixture. Top with the remaining sauce and Kinder bars to decorate.

4. Place the lid on the tub and freeze for a minimum of 6 hours.

5. Once frozen, leave out for 5 to 10 minutes before serving. Scoop out and enjoy with your favourite toppings, like one of our Dolly's Luxury Dessert Sauces.

Dolly's
DESSERTS

Cherry Bakewell Ice Cream

This old school recipe lends itself so well to ice cream. Try serving with vanilla cake, whipped cream, Dolly's White Chocolate Sauce and extra glacé cherries for a stunning sundae!

PREP TIME: 15 MINUTES, PLUS 6 HOURS FREEZING | COOKING TIME: 10 MINUTES | MAKES APPROX. 1KG

Ingredients

350g frozen cherries

70g caster sugar

6 digestive biscuits

20g unsalted butter, melted

480ml whipping cream

1 x 397g tin of condensed milk (best chilled)

1 tsp almond essence

150g flaked almonds, plus 50g to decorate

Glacé cherries, to decorate

Method

1. Place the frozen cherries and sugar in a small saucepan and cook on a medium heat until the sugar has dissolved and the mixture has thickened. Remove from the heat and set aside to cool.

2. Crush the digestives into crumbs, stir in the melted butter, then set aside.

3. Add the cream to a bowl and whisk on full power using an electric whisk until stiff peaks form.

4. Add the condensed milk and almond essence to the bowl and whisk on low power until incorporated.

5. Gently fold in the cooled, cooked cherries and 150g of flaked almonds, then transfer to a freezer-safe container and smooth out to the edges.

6. Top with the remaining flaked almonds and decorate with glacé cherries.

7. Wrap with cling film to ensure no moisture can enter, then chill in the freezer for a minimum of 6 hours.

8. Leave out for 5 to 10 minutes before serving.

Rich Chocolate Ice Cream

Sometimes all you need is a simple scoop of chocolate ice cream, and this recipe is way easier than you think! Pop a scoop between two chocolate chip cookies for the perfect ice cream cookie sandwich.

PREP TIME: 15 MINUTES, PLUS 6 HOURS FREEZING | COOKING TIME: 5 MINUTES | MAKES APPROX. 1KG

Ingredients

100g cocoa powder

180ml full fat milk

480ml whipping cream

1 x 397g tin of condensed milk (best chilled)

200g dark chocolate, finely chopped

Method

1. Add the cocoa powder and milk to a pan and gently warm. Stir until it forms a really smooth and rich paste, then set aside to cool.

2. Add the cream to a bowl and whisk on full power using an electric whisk until stiff peaks form.

3. Add the condensed milk and chocolate paste and whisk on low power until incorporated. Fold through 150g of the chopped chocolate, then scoop the mixture into a freezer-safe container.

4. Smooth out to the edges, then top with the remaining chopped chocolate.

5. Wrap with cling film to ensure no moisture can enter, then chill in the freezer for a minimum of 6 hours.

6. Leave out for 5 to 10 minutes before serving with your favourite toppings, like one (or more) of our Dolly's Luxury Dessert Sauces.

Chocolate Caramel Brownie Ice Cream

Can't decide whether to have a brownie or some ice cream? Have both! This recipe looks so good scooped into a glass and topped with caramel and Dolly's Milk Chocolate Sauce. Add finely chopped dark chocolate for an extra-fancy finish.

PREP TIME: 15 MINUTES, PLUS 6 HOURS FREEZING | COOKING TIME: 5 MINUTES | MAKES APPROX. 1KG

Ingredients

100ml full fat milk

60g cocoa powder

480ml whipping cream

1 x 397g tin of condensed milk (best chilled)

Brownies, chopped, plus extra to decorate (we use three of our OG brownies, page 74, but follow your heart/stomach on this one!)

200-300g Caramel Spread (see page 187)

Method

1. In a small saucepan, warm the milk and cocoa powder until fully combined, then set aside to cool.

2. Add the cream to a bowl and whisk on full power using an electric whisk until stiff peaks form.

3. Add the condensed milk and cooled cocoa to the bowl, then whisk on low power until incorporated.

4. Fold some chopped brownie pieces through the mixture, then scoop it into a freezer-safe container. Ripple with Caramel Spread and smooth out to the edges.

5. Top with extra brownie pieces and Caramel Spread, then wrap with cling film to ensure no moisture can enter. Chill in the freezer for a minimum of 6 hours to set.

6. Leave out for 5 to 10 minutes before serving with your choice of extra toppings.

Peanut Butter Ice Cream

If you really want to turn this into something special, stir through some chocolate spread, and serve each scoop with half a Snickers bar and a healthy drizzle of chocolate sauce.

PREP TIME: 15 MINUTES, PLUS 6 HOURS FREEZING | COOKING TIME: 5 MINUTES | MAKES APPROX. 1KG

Ingredients

480ml whipping cream

350g peanut butter

1 x 397g tin of condensed milk (best chilled)

200g salted peanuts, chopped

Method

1. Add the cream to a bowl and whisk on full power using an electric whisk until stiff peaks form.

2. Add the peanut butter to a bowl and microwave for 20 seconds until melted (but not molten - leave to cool a little if it's too hot to the touch).

3. Add the condensed milk and 300g of the melted peanut butter to the cream and whisk on low power until fully incorporated.

4. Scoop the mixture into a freezer-safe container and layer with the remaining 50g of peanut butter and the chopped peanuts. Create ripples through the ice cream using a skewer or sharp knife.

5. Smooth out to the edges then top with more chopped nuts, if desired.

6. Wrap with cling film to ensure no moisture can enter, then chill in the freezer for a minimum of 6 hours.

7. Leave out for 5 to 10 minutes before serving with your favourite toppings, like one (or more) of our Dolly's Luxury Dessert Sauces.

Strawberry Ice Cream

A classic fruity flavour that we use in a few of our recipes. Try it in our super creamy Strawberry Shortcake Freakshake (see page 48) or our nostalgic fave, Banana Split (see page 86). I mean, how can you not love strawberry ice cream?

PREP TIME: 15 MINUTES, PLUS 6 HOURS FREEZING | COOKING TIME: 1 HOUR | MAKES APPROX. 1.5KG

Ingredients

750g fresh strawberries

1 tbsp white sugar

1 tsp vanilla extract

480ml whipping cream

1 x 397g tin of condensed milk (best chilled)

Method

1. Preheat the oven to 170°c, then put the strawberries on a lined baking tray and sprinkle with the sugar.

2. Roast for 45 minutes, turning the tray halfway through. Then, remove from the oven, add the vanilla, give the strawberries a good shake, and return to the oven for 15 minutes. Keep an eye on them as you don't want the juices to turn to strawberry toffee!

3. Remove the roasted strawberries from the oven, blitz in a blender and set aside to cool completely.

4. Add the cream to a bowl and whisk on full power using an electric whisk until stiff peaks form.

5. Add the blitzed strawberries and condensed milk to the bowl, then whisk on low power until incorporated.

6. Scoop the mixture into a freezer-safe container and smooth out to the edges.

7. Cover with cling film to ensure no moisture can enter, then chill in the freezer to set for at least 6 hours.

8. Leave out to soften for 5 to 10 minutes before scooping and serving.

Dolly's
Dolly's
DESSERTS

Cookies & Cream Cheesecake Ice Cream

This one's a really popular flavour for all the family. We just love how the Oreo cookies blend into the ice cream to create a beautiful marbled effect.

PREP TIME: 15 MINUTES, PLUS 6 HOURS FREEZING | MAKES APPROX. 1KG

Ingredients

10 Oreos or similar cookies and cream biscuits

240ml whipping cream

240ml sour cream

1 x 397g tin of condensed milk (best chilled)

80g cream cheese

Method

1. Smash the Oreo cookies into pieces using a rolling pin, being careful to leave some larger pieces.

2. Add both creams to a mixing bowl and whisk on full power using an electric whisk until stiff peaks form.

3. Add the condensed milk and cream cheese to the bowl and whisk on low power until incorporated.

4. Fold the crushed cookies through the mixture, then scoop it into a freezer-safe container and smooth out to the edges. Sprinkle with more crushed cookies, if you like.

5. Wrap with cling film to ensure no moisture can enter, then put in the freezer for a minimum of 6 hours.

6. Leave out for 5 to 10 minutes before serving with your favourite toppings, like one (or more) of our Dolly's Luxury Dessert Sauces.

Strawberry Cheesecake Ice Cream

This recipe can easily be adapted to use any seasonal berry. Blackberries, blueberries, raspberries, the list goes on - just switch out the strawberries and you're done! You can also use frozen berries - just thaw them slightly first so the sugar doesn't burn in the pan before the fruit breaks down.

PREP TIME: 15 MINUTES, PLUS 6 HOURS FREEZING | COOKING TIME: 10 MINUTES | MAKES APPROX. 1KG

Ingredients

340g fresh strawberries, chopped small

70g caster sugar

1 ½ tsp vanilla extract

200g digestive biscuits

45g butter, melted

480ml whipping cream

80g sour cream

1 x 397g tin of condensed milk (best chilled)

160g cream cheese

Method

1. Add the strawberries, sugar and vanilla to a pan and cook on a medium heat until the sugar has dissolved and the mixture has thickened. Remove from the heat and set aside to cool.

2. Bash the digestive biscuits to make fine crumbs and stir in the melted butter. Set aside.

3. Add both creams to a bowl and whisk on full power using an electric whisk until stiff peaks form.

4. Add the condensed milk and cream cheese to the bowl and whisk on low power until incorporated, then carefully fold in the cooled, cooked strawberries and biscuit crumb. Do this in stages and be careful to not over-stir it - you want evenly distributed ripples.

5. Scoop the mixture into a freezer-safe container, then wrap with cling film to ensure no moisture can enter. Chill in the freezer for 6 hours or until set.

6. Leave out for 5 to 10 minutes to soften before serving.

Vanilla Ice Cream

We know it's not exactly the same as the one we make in store because that requires expensive machinery, but this simple recipe is by far the best (not to mention the quickest and most adaptable). We use whipping cream as we prefer the lighter texture, but you can use double cream for a more dense, creamy result!

PREP TIME: 15 MINUTES, PLUS 6 HOURS FREEZING | MAKES APPROX. 1KG

Ingredients

480ml whipping cream

1 fresh vanilla pod, seeds removed, or 1 tsp vanilla extract

1 x 397g tin of condensed milk (best chilled)

Method

1. Add the cream to a bowl and whisk on full power using an electric whisk until stiff peaks form.

2. Add the vanilla extract or, if using, split the vanilla pod down the centre and scrape out the vanilla seeds.

3. Add the condensed milk to the bowl and whisk on low power until incorporated.

4. Scoop the mixture into a freezer-safe container and smooth out to the edges. Wrap with cling film to ensure no moisture can enter, then chill in the freezer for a minimum of 6 hours.

5. To serve, leave out for 5 to 10 minutes to soften before scooping into bowls. Enjoy with your favourite toppings, like one (or more) of our Dolly's Luxury Dessert Sauces.

Pampered Pups

We had to include something in our book for the absolute superstars of our family, Dolly and Rupert. Yes, we know Dolly already has a dessert shop named after her, but she was the first child! Rupert wasn't even a twinkle in our eyes when Dolly's started. Who knows, maybe one day he will become just as famous. If you love your doggies as much as we do, daily treats are a must, and this section is definitely for you!

Rupert's Ripple

We love the ripples in these - they're as golden as Rupert's fur (so, of course, these are also his favourite!). Why not double up on the peanut butter and coconut oil ripple and pour it into mini bun cases? You can top them with crushed peanuts to make extra-special pup cups!

PREP TIME: 20 MINUTES, PLUS 6 HOURS FREEZING | MAKES 500G

Ingredients

3 ripe bananas

30g coconut oil, melted

1 x 400ml tin full fat coconut milk, chilled

65g natural, unsweetened peanut butter

Method

1. Slice the bananas into half-inch pieces and lay on a lined or greased chopping board. Freeze for about an hour until solid.

2. Melt the coconut oil for a few seconds in the microwave, then place the chilled coconut milk, frozen bananas and 10g of the coconut oil in a blender and blend to a smooth consistency.

3. Melt the peanut butter and combine with the remaining coconut oil to form a smooth, golden sauce.

4. Pour half the coconut and banana mixture into a freezer-safe container, around the size of a loaf tin, then drizzle half the peanut butter sauce into the mixture. Swirl it around with a skewer or pointy knife, then repeat this process to create two rippled layers.

5. Cover with cling film and freeze for 5 hours. This recipe will last for at least 3 months in the freezer.

Tip: Try freezing a clean dog KONG for 30 minutes and filling it with some of Rupert's Ripple for an extra-cold treat on a hot summer's day!

Dolly's Biscuit Bones

Make no bones about it, Dolly just loves these! They're always a welcome addition to the treat jar!

Ingredients

200g oats

100g seeds (pumpkin or sunflower)

75g unsweetened apple sauce

40g olive oil

Method

1. Preheat the oven to 180°c and grease and line a baking tray.
2. Grind the oats and seeds together using a blender or food processor to make a fine powder.
3. Stir in the apple sauce and oil and knead together to form a firm dough.
4. Dust the worktop with a little flour and roll out the dough to about 0.5cm thick, then use a bone-shaped cutter (or whatever shape you like) to cut out biscuits.
5. Space the biscuits out on the baking tray and bake for 20 minutes until hardened and cooked through.
6. Allow to cool before storing in an airtight container for 3 weeks.

Barking Brownies

These delicious brownies for dogs are made with carob powder, which is a delicious, dog-friendly alternative to cocoa powder. Did you know that carob powder also contains a sprinkling of fibre, potassium and essential vitamins? Who said brownies couldn't be healthy?

PREP TIME: 10 MINUTES, PLUS 3 HOURS CHILLING | COOKING TIME: 20 MINUTES

Ingredients

4 eggs

2 tbsp honey

1 tsp vanilla extract

40g vegetable oil

125g wholewheat flour

35g carob powder

65g carob chips

Method

1. Preheat the oven to 180°c and line a baking tin with greaseproof paper.

2. Add eggs, honey, vanilla and oil to a mixing bowl and whisk well.

3. Sift in the wholewheat flour and carob powder and whisk until fully combined.

4. Fold in the carob chips then transfer the batter to the baking tin.

5. Gently tap the tin on the counter to help distribute the batter evenly, then pop in the oven for 20 minutes. In the meantime, let your fur baby lick the bowl clean (obviously).

6. Once the brownie is cooked through, set aside to cool. (To check whether it's cooked, pop a skewer or fork into the centre of the brownie - if it comes out clean, it's cooked.)

7. Refrigerate for 3 hours before slicing and serving to your pup.

Tip: Don't forget to adjust your dog's food slightly on the days you give them this treat to prevent overeating.

Fillings & Spreads

Although we are partial to buying a spread or filling, we also love to make them ourselves! Here are a few essential fillings and spreads to take your recipes to the next level! If you haven't got time, you can always buy some as a substitute - we won't tell!

White Chocolate Spread

This one's used in lots of our recipes as it's the perfect filling for cookie pies, stuffed cookies or even on your toast if you're feeling fancy!

COOKING TIME: 10 MINUTES | MAKES 350G

Ingredients

100g white chocolate, roughly chopped (or chips)

100g unsalted butter

150g sweetened condensed milk

2 pinches of sea salt

Method

1. Add all the ingredients to a saucepan and stir over a low heat until melted.

2. Keep stirring vigorously to bring it together and make sure the butter is well incorporated.

3. Pour into an airtight container and store in the fridge until the spread hardens.

4. Use this as cookie fillings, on top of millionaires shortbread or even on your breakfast!

Caramel Spread

The most delicious sticky caramel ever! We have tried to make it multiple ways, but we've found this one works perfectly every time.

PREP TIME: 5 MINUTES | COOKING TIME: 25 MINUTES | MAKES APPROX. 700G

Ingredients

350g caster sugar

70ml water

200g double cream

90g unsalted butter

Pinch of sea salt (optional)

Method

1. Add the sugar and water to a saucepan and stir over a medium heat until the sugar dissolves.

2. Leave the sugar syrup on a medium heat until it turns an amber colour. Do not stir it! We know you want to! But just trust us!

3. Once the sugar is a deep amber in colour and bubbling, remove it from the heat and carefully pour in the double cream. This is going to cause the caramel to bubble a lot and go a little crazy, but do not worry - just keep stirring it in until it's combined.

4. Once the bubbling stops, add the butter and stir until it's melted and fully incorporated. If you like, stir in a good pinch of sea salt.

5. Pour the caramel into a heatproof container and allow to cool before popping it in the fridge to set. Once set, store it in the fridge for up to 3 months!

Edible Cookie Dough

This is a staple for a lot of our recipes in the book! Whether you're using it for ice cream or brownies or eating it from the bowl, you definitely need to give it a try!

PREP TIME: 10 MINUTES | COOKING TIME: 10 MINUTES | MAKES APPROX. 1KG

Ingredients

250g plain flour

230g salted butter

150g light soft brown sugar

150g caster sugar

1 tbsp double cream

1 tsp vanilla extract

300g chocolate, roughly chopped, or chocolate chips (we like to use a bit of dark and milk)

Method

1. Spread the flour onto a baking tray and bake at 190ºc for 10 minutes (this is an essential step as uncooked flour can carry harmful bacteria). Set aside to cool.

2. Place the butter into the microwave for 20 seconds or until half melted. This will help dissolve the sugar and produce a less gritty texture.

3. In a bowl, add both sugars and the part-melted butter. Mix with an electric whisk or spatula until smooth and combined. Add the vanilla and double cream and stir together.

4. Add the roughly chopped chocolate or chocolate chips into the bowl and fold until combined.

5. Carefully add the cooled flour and fold it in until the mixture forms dough. Don't be scared to get your hands in to give it a good mix!

6. This can be eaten as it is, baked to be eaten warm, or stored in the fridge for up to 5 days. You can even freeze it for up to 2 months!

Simple Shortbread

Four ingredients: you really can't go wrong. This buttery bake is a perfect base
for our millionaires shortbread recipes, but if you're into the classics then it's just
as good to eat as it is!

PREP TIME: 5 MINUTES | MAKES 360G

Ingredients

125g good quality unsalted butter, softened

55g caster sugar

180g plain flour

Pinch of salt

Method

1. In a large mixing bowl, cream the butter and sugar until smooth.
2. Sift in the flour and salt, then mix until it forms a smooth dough.
3. Roll out the dough and cut it into the desired portions or press into the base of a baking tin to form the base of any of our millionaires recipes!

Cookie Crumb Mix

Here you have the perfect cookie crumb mix. It's great for cheesecake bases or
sprinkled on top of ice creams or pancakes! We use this so much at Dolly's – our
customers love it as a topping.

PREP TIME: 5 MINUTES | MAKES 300G

Ingredients

250g digestive biscuits

50g salted butter, melted

Method

1. Add the digestive biscuits to a sealable sandwich bag and smash them with a rolling pin. You want to keep smashing until there are no large pieces of biscuit left.
2. Add to a bowl along with the melted butter, then mix until combined. Use immediately or store in an airtight container for up to 2 months.

Dolly's Desserts

©2024 Dolly's Desserts &
Meze Publishing Limited

First edition printed in 2024 in
the UK

ISBN: 9781915538291

Written by: Charlie Smark and
Janine Davies

Edited by: Emily Readman

Photography by:
Timm Cleasby

Designed by:
Paul Cocker and Phil Turner

PR and Sales: Emma Toogood

Contributors:
Cara Snowden,

Ben Doyle, Sophia Derby

Printed and bound in the UK
by Bell & Bain Ltd, Glasgow

Published by Meze Publishing Ltd
Unit 1b, 2 Kelham Square
Kelham Riverside
Sheffield S3 8SD

Web: www.mezepublishing.co.uk

Telephone: 0114 275 7709

Email: info@mezepublishing.co.uk

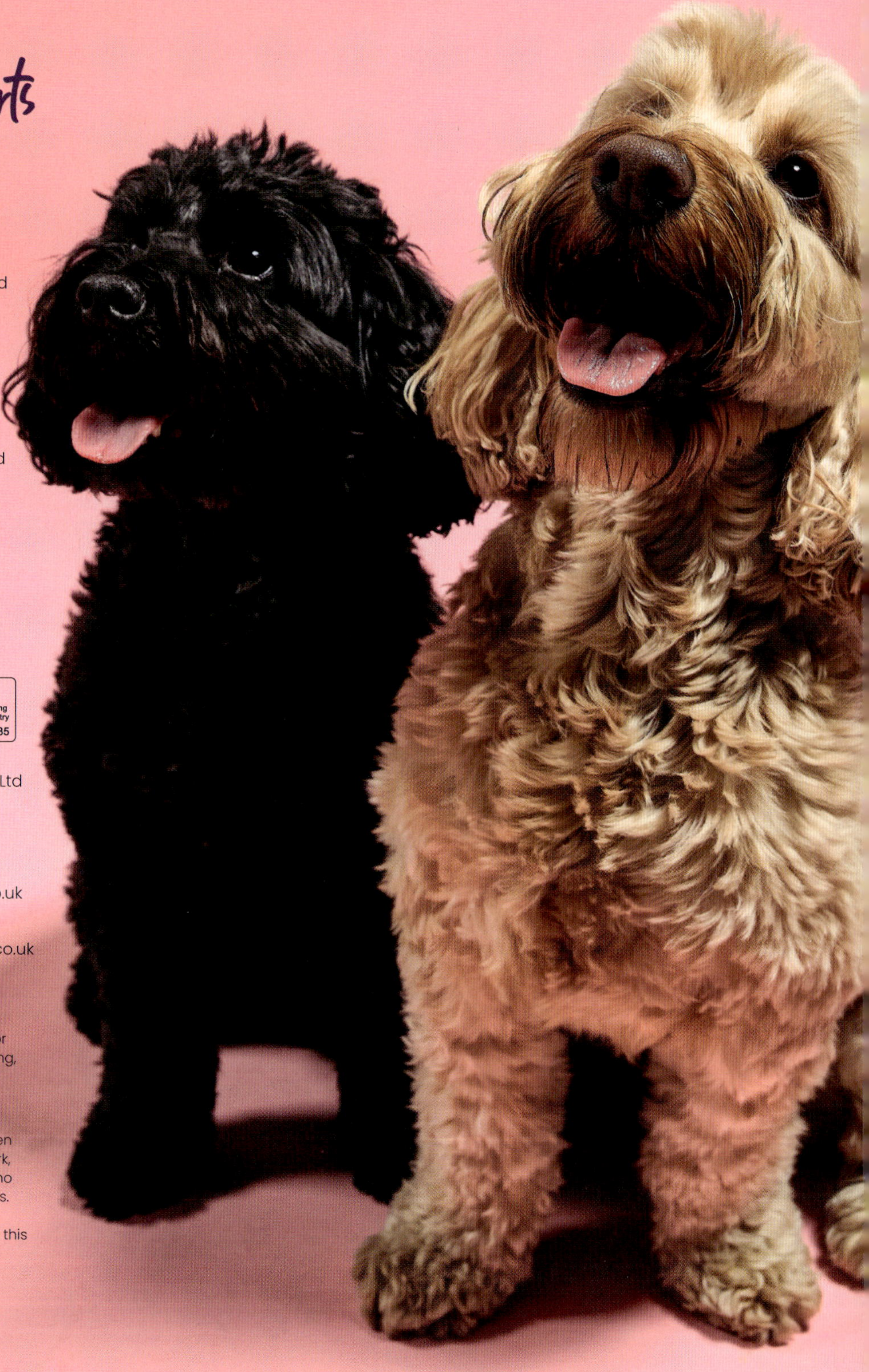